SUSTAINABLE GENEALOGY:

SEPARATING FACT FROM FICTION IN FAMILY LEGENDS

BY

RICHARD HITE

With a Foreword by Henry Z Jones, Jr.
Fellow, American Society of Genealogists

Published by Genealogical Publishing Company
3600 Clipper Mill Rd., #260
Baltimore, Maryland 21211-1953

Library of Congress Catalog Card Number 2013949937
ISBN 978-0-8063-1982-7

Made in the United States of America

In Memoriam

Jessie Rebecca (Bagley) Hite (1900-1985)

Melba (Grogan) Williams (1909-1987)

My first sources of oral history

John C. Rosser, Jr. (1933-2001)

My first instructor in genealogy

Table of Contents

Illustrations

Foreword

Genealogists today are living in some interesting times. We have a wealth of new tools and toys to play with, making our research easier and quicker. With the internet accessible in every home and local library, family historians now can access sources that would have been difficult to locate before *and* network and compare notes with other genealogists around the world who are working on the same families.

But besides being a blessing, the internet is also a curse: shoddy research abounds, undocumented family connectives are widespread, and spurious sources often outnumber the legitimate ones. Unproven family traditions often are accepted unconditionally as fact and then, worst of all, venture down the internet highway, eventually making them seem like gospel rather than the garbage they really are.

Many of the genealogical sources used today derive from the oral histories passed down in families for generations, which were subsequently published in the "Mug Books" and other local histories that flourished in the late 19th and early 20th centuries. They thus have evolved into "written oral histories," one of the several important subjects focused on by Richard Hite in this book.

I know of no one better suited to write a book on "sustainable genealogy" than Richard, inasmuch as the Hite Family Tree has branches that are textbook examples of how family tradition—as opposed to evidence--sometimes can lead us far astray from our actual genealogy. For the past fifty years, I have immersed myself in documenting, tracing, and then writing about the myriad German "Palatine" emigrants who settled in colonial America in the 18th century. Of the 847 Palatine families who settled first in New York in 1710, the Hites included in this group held no special interest for me personally, as I descended from none of the 847 myself. However, I gradually learned that the Hites were a somewhat unique and special case: their progenitor was Jost Hite, the so-called "Baron of the Shenandoah Valley," a friend of George Washington and one of the largest and wealthiest landholders in that region. His descendants called him "Baron Hite," believing he had possessed a noble background in Europe prior to his arrival in the new world.

I looked for Jost Hite's overseas origins in just the same way as I looked for all the other families with whom he travelled; the methodology I developed of studying all the emigrants in *clusters* of families enabled me to finally document over 600 of the 847 Palatines in their ancestral homes in Europe. It turned out that "Baron" Jost Hite was not a Baron at all, but instead the son of the town butcher of Bonfeld, Germany. Richard, in his position as President and Chief Genealogist of the thriving Hite Family Association, over many years was able to build upon my findings with new data, and then separate other, different Hite family groups (including his own ancestors) from Jost's proven line. "

Richard's critical eagle-eye served him well in this task. He was fighting the old "Well if my last name is Boone, I *must* be a descendant of Daniel Boone" syndrome that pops up so often in our field. Like a skilled surgeon, he took out his genealogical scalpel nd dissected some of the erroneous Hite family traditions to separate fiction from fact and thus Jost from some of the other completely different, later-arriving Hite lines. This book covers the methodology he used, the questions he asked, and – most important of all - how his wisdom might help YOU as you climb your own family tree.

You'll find lots of genealogical bases beyond Hite lore covered here: how sometimes the origins of certain families are attributed to the wrong ethnic group; how the very common two or three immigrant brothers tradition and their geographic dispersal is often attributed to the wrong side of the family tree; what to do when even the primary sources are in error; how Native American ancestry is fun to talk about, but hard to prove; and on and on in fascinating detail.

Reading Richard's thoughts and experiences cannot help but lead you into taking a more critical look at the accuracy and veracity of the sources you use to compile your own family's genealogy. I guarantee you that taking heed of the cautions cited and putting into practice the lessons learned in this book will make you all much better family historians and ensure that your genealogical legacy will be one to be trusted.

Henry Z Jones, Jr.
Fellow,
American Society of Genealogists
28 August 2013

Introduction

It was August of 1979. My father, John L. Hite, and I, having just begun research on our family genealogy two months earlier, were attending a reunion of a prominent Hite family in Virginia's Shenandoah Valley – a family we had no idea if we were related to or not. The reunion event we were most anticipating was the Family History Roundtable that was scheduled for a Saturday afternoon. It was at that event that I first learned how badly flawed oral history could be – and also how much passion revelations of those flaws could generate.

The Hite family associated with the Shenandoah Valley (the most prominent one of several we later learned) could trace its lineage to Jost Hite, who had risen to prominence in the Valley after leading a migration of numerous families of German descent from eastern Pennsylvania to this newly opened frontier in the early 1730s. The first few generations of his descendants continued to be community powerbrokers after his lifetime. Numerous oral and written accounts of this man claimed that he had held the title of "Baron" in his German homeland prior to coming to the American colonies, that he was a native of the area in or around the city of Strasbourg in modern-day France, and that his wife was Anna Maria Dubois of a wealthy Huguenot family whom he had met only after fleeing Germany when his family estates were overrun by marauding French soldiers. Unbeknownst to my dad and me, Jost Hite's true origins had been discovered by professional researchers in Germany just a year or two prior to that time and had been published earlier that same year. As revealed by Hank Jones, now famous for his numerous publications on the large migration of Germans to England in 1709 and then on to other locations (primarily the American colonies), Jost Hite (baptized Hans Justus Heyd) was actually a native of the village of Bonfeld in the Kraichgau region of Germany, born there in 1685. His father was not a Baron, but a butcher, and by the time of his marriage, in the village of his birth, Jost himself was a weaver by trade. His wife, whom he married at the unusually young age of eighteen, was not a Huguenot named Dubois, but was instead Anna Maria Merckle, born in the same village in 1687 to parents no more prominent than Jost's own.

The outcry against these research results I heard at this reunion still amazes me to this day, and Dad and I continued to joke about it on occasion until his death in 2003. I have often wondered if Hank Jones would have escaped a lynching had he attended that reunion. Klaus Wust, a professional historian who had collaborated with Jones in his work[1], did attend and he certainly received more than his share of hostility from the audience as he addressed them. In conversations with other attendees after the presentation, Dad and I encountered several who absolutely refused to believe that their long held traditions about Jost Hite and his wife were inaccurate. None of that mattered much to us – we only wanted to know if we were from Jost Hite's family or not – regardless of what his true origins were. Within a year after that reunion,

---

[1] Klaus Wust, "Postscript: Chasing an Alsatian Baron" in Henry Z. Jones, Ralph, Connor, Klaus Wust, *German Origins of Jost Hite, Virginia Pioneer* (Edinburg, VA: Shenandoah History Publishers, 1979), pp. 27-30.

we definitively proved that we were not descendants of Jost Hite, but we continued, in later years, to attend those reunions. As is usually the case with researchers who discover a family's true origins, most descendants eventually accept the results of the work. In 1994, Hank Jones was invited to speak at the reunion banquet, and at the end of his presentation, he received a standing ovation. He is now a hero to most of them and more than a few have visited Jost Hite's ancestral village of Bonfeld, where his childhood home still stands. Those few who have refused to accept the primary source documentation of their ancestral home have missed out on learning their true heritage, while those who have accepted it have learned that it is every bit as interesting as the discredited oral traditions.

More than thirty years later, I have lost count of the number of oral traditions that have fallen by the wayside under the lens of careful research in primary sources and more recently, DNA testing. This is true not only of my own ancestral families, but also in the families of many friends and acquaintances as well as prominent public figures. I do not, however, mourn these "losses" for the simple reason I do not see them as losses. To paraphrase an old quote that "truth is stranger than fiction", I have come to believe that truth is more interesting than fiction.

My late grandmothers, Jessie Rebecca (Bagley) Hite and Melba (Grogan) Williams were my first sources of oral history. They were both alive and mentally alert when I began researching my own genealogy in the late 1970s. Grandma Hite was always a little mystified at my interest, but she nonetheless shared everything she knew. My grandmother Williams seemed to understand my interest a bit more – she had talked a bit about family history when I was younger and shared my interest to some degree. During their lifetimes and after they were dead, I proved some of the things they had told me and disproved others. I am hard-pressed to remember anything either of them told me, however, that did not lead me to something useful even if it was not perfectly accurate. There were others of their generation I talked to that added to the information I got from them and, in some cases, conflicted with what my grandmothers had told me. Again, some was right and some was wrong, but all of it was useful. To them, and to my grandmothers, I owe an undying debt of gratitude.

I also must mention the influence of my late cousin, John C. Rosser, Jr. (1933-2001), who taught me what not to take for granted in genealogy work. From him, I learned the pitfalls of accepting everything in published county histories and in printed genealogies. Much of this material, though written, must be considered oral history, or legend, because that is what it was based on. Another cousin, Robert W. Carter, Jr., augmented this lesson with the research he shared.

Throughout this work, I cite examples of oral histories in various families, most of them my own ancestors, although some involve neighbors of my ancestors or the ancestors of public figures. I also included some several stories I learned from friends about their family traditions.

I would like to thank Jennifer Stevens, Sheri Cole Norton, Karl Baughman, and the late Danny L. Miller for sharing their families' traditions with me for inclusion in this work.

I would also like to thank my cousin David Dinwiddie, who came to my rescue as this project was drawing to a close, when I needed help with the technological aspects of the final preparations. David has long shared my interest in our shared family history and I am eternally grateful for the assistance he provided me over those last several days.

Finally, I have to acknowledge the aforementioned Hank Jones, from whom I first learned how so many similar oral traditions are found in family after family. After all, wasn't every colonial American family founded by three brothers, all of whom married Cherokee princesses? Wasn't this true despite the fact that these three men with the same surname arrived in three distinct regions of the colonies over a period of fifty years? Wasn't it true despite the fact that none of them ever lived within two hundred miles of any Cherokee villages? Finally, wasn't it true despite the fact that the wives they had married in Europe before their emigrations outlived them? I can only hope that my own experiences in separating fact from fiction can guide others in their efforts to achieve the same goal.

Chapter 1 - Recurring Patterns in Oral History

Anyone who develops an interest in genealogy is always told "Talk to Grandma". "Talk to Grandpa." "Find out what they know." Sound advice, no doubt. After all, Grandma and Grandpa (or whoever the oldest living family members are) usually knew some of the people one is interested in and they remember some events that happened in previous years. But, after talking to these people, it's never a good idea to just blindly accept what they said and use that as a starting point. Instead, one should go to other sources such as vital statistics, census records, church records, and whatever else is available to verify what these people said. Then one should proceed from there.

"Written" Oral History

What our older family members told us is usually what we define as oral history and it is the most common form of it. However, much of what is written must also be lumped into the category of oral history (an appropriate term is "written oral history"). Perhaps the best example of this is published county histories, many of which appeared in print throughout the United States from the 1870s until the years immediately preceding World War I. Why is this oral history, one might ask? That's certainly a valid question when it is, after all, in print. The reason for this is simple – many of the biographical accounts of particular individuals found in these books are taken from informal interviews with them or their next-of-kin. Often, these accounts give names of, and information about, distant ancestors of these people. In many cases, these ancestors had died well before the lifetimes of the subjects of the biographies. The subjects were relying only on what they were told by their older family members. It cannot be assumed that they went to the local courthouses, or made trips to courthouses in the areas their ancestors came from to research their own backgrounds. In fact, it is quite safe to assume that very few people in the late 19th and early 20th centuries had the time and the financial means to do all this, even if they were interested. Anything in these biographical accounts that involves people the subjects knew, such as their parents, is generally fairly reliable, though it should be verified with primary sources. But accounts of grandparents and great-grandparents, who died before the lifetimes of the subjects or when the subjects were young children, demand verification. No one today has a perfect memory. It cannot be assumed that our ancestors of a century ago had better memories than we did.

Much of what we see on the Internet today also has to be lumped into the category of oral history, even though it is written. On sites like Genforum, Rootsweb, and Ancestry.com, I have seen all kinds of accounts of ancestors that are obviously not supported by documentation. Much of it contradicts itself and for families I have researched myself, I have seen links repeated that were published in county histories, but disproved long ago by research in primary sources. Most people view the Internet as a wonderful boon to genealogy. It does have its advantages in that it facilitates communication among genealogists and allows distant relatives who are interested in family connections to find each other more easily. Certainly, some of the family accounts that are posted are quite good. But in other ways, the Internet has set genealogy back thirty years. The main reason for this is that a whole new generation of people who may have always had an interest, but never had the energy or the means to go out and research for themselves now have a huge amount of information at their fingertips. A number of family legends from county histories and other secondary sources have found their way onto the Internet. Much of it is simply unverified oral history.

I am by no means suggesting that genealogists should discount what their older relatives have told them or other forms of oral history. Very often, research in primary sources verifies what is told in this history or at least shows that there are elements of truth in it. The mistake that far too many genealogists make is to assume that all of this information is accurate in all of its details. This can lead them to ignore primary sources. In other cases, it can lead them to focus their research too narrowly when consulting primary sources.

I was often guilty of this myself in the early stages of my research. One of my first mistakes was to accept without question some names on a chart my father had prepared when talking to my grandmother about her family. He had written the name of one of her great-grandfathers as James Hamilton. My grandmother, Jessie Rebecca (Bagley) Hite, was born in 1900 in Columbus Township, Warren County, Pennsylvania and I understood that her mother, Matilda Lovisa (Bush) Bagley, had grown up in the same vicinity. When I first checked for them in the 1850 census, I found Matilda's parents, Alonzo and Mary Bush, in the very township my grandmother had been born in. Living nearby were Alonzo's parents, Joshua and Lovisa Bush. This was my first clue that my father's chart was not entirely accurate. He had identified Joshua Bush's wife as Matilda Abbey and the wife of James Hamilton (the supposed father of Mary Bush) as Lovisa Ingersoll. But, I assumed, he or my grandmother had simply mixed the two wives up. I still did not doubt that James Hamilton was Mary Bush's father, even when I did not find anyone of that name in Warren County. I looked back at the 1850 census index for Pennsylvania and found a James Hamilton listed in Venango County, Pennsylvania – a county that bordered Warren County to the southwest. I looked him up and saw that he was 60 years old – a perfect age to be the father of Mary Bush who was then 27. His wife was not named Matilda, but that was no matter, I thought. His first wife Matilda had probably died and he had remarried – that was the logical conclusion, especially since his then-wife Margaret was nineteen years younger than him. I was sure I had found my great-great-great-grandfather and soon after, I found an account in a published history of Venango County that identified James, his father (also named James) and his grandfather Thomas Hamilton, the latter two of whom were natives of Ireland.[1] I had done it! This was the first of my immigrant ancestors on my father's side that I had been able to identify.

Both Those Awful Names!

This was not a time in my life that I could dedicate to genealogy, however. I was a freshman in college. My grandmother was still living, but it was three years before I

---

[1] Charles Almanzo Babcock, *Venango County, Pennsylvania: Her Pioneers and People, Embracing a General History of the County, and a Genealogical and Biographical Record of Representative Families* (Chicago: J.H. Beers, 1919), p. 347-348.

saw her again. When I got the chance, I showed her the census listing I had copied with the names of James Hamilton's children who had still been living at home at the time (her great-aunts and great-uncles, I assumed, and I thought she might remember some of them). She just kept shaking her head. "Those names just don't sound right," she kept saying, over and over. "Venango County. It just doesn't sound right." She also kept mentioning repeatedly that her grandmother Bush had been a Quaker. This was surprising to me, because there was no mention in the published history of the family of James Hamilton that indicated a Quaker connection. She also kept mentioning the names of both of her maternal great-grandmothers (Matilda and Lovisa) and pointed out "My mother got stuck with both those awful names!" which was true. I finally asked if she remembered the name of her grandmother's father. After thinking for a couple of minutes she responded, "I believe it was Charles." Well, right then, I was sure I had probably researched the wrong family.

Eventually, my research led me to Mary's actual parents – Moses (not James *or* Charles) *Hambleton* and Matilda Sherman (not Abbey). They were living in the town of Ellery in Chautauqua County, New York at the time of the 1850 census which is actually closer to Columbus Township than Venango County is despite being in a different state. They were, indeed, Quakers, just as my grandmother had said. So she was not entirely wrong the first time. However, she was not entirely right either. I had learned my lesson about taking everything she and my other older relatives told me for granted. I had learned to prove (or disprove) what they said first and then follow whatever path my research took me down.

Whom Did They Know?

It is not always easy to distinguish fact from fiction in oral history. There are, however, certain guidelines one can follow in terms of guessing how accurate a family story an older relative told is likely to be. We must ask ourselves several questions:
1.   Did the informant know the people involved?
2.   If so, how old was the informant when the people involved died?
3.   Whether or not the informant knew them, did he or she grow up in the same vicinity as the people in the story?
In the case of my grandmother, she did not know her grandmother, Mary (Hambleton) Bush, who died in 1881, nineteen years before Grandma was born. She *did* spend her early childhood in the same area that her grandparents had lived in as adults and may have known some of her grandmother's siblings. She was right about the Quaker connection, but she was wrong about the first name of her great-grandfather Moses Hambleton and also about the spelling of her grandmother's maiden name (she had probably only heard it and never saw it written, so it is understandable that she remembered it as *Hamilton*). It is noteworthy that she did correctly remember the first name of Moses Hambleton's wife Matilda. The reason for that is obvious. Her own mother had been named Matilda, for this grandmother, and evidently often mentioned that she had been named for both grandmothers, a fact that her daughter Jessie knew very well. Jessie had not correctly remembered Matilda Hambleton's maiden name, but that name had not been incorporated into Matilda Bush's name, so it was less significant.

3

Biographical accounts in county histories should be subjected to similar criteria. A discerning genealogist will first check the date of publication and then address the following questions:

1. Which of the people mentioned in the account were living at the time of publication?
2. Which ones mentioned as ancestors of the subject lived into his/her lifetime?
3. Which ones are described as having lived in or near the area the subject lived in?
4. How glamorous is the account of the subject's ancestors? (If it seems overly glamorized, it has to be examined particularly closely. Particularly questionable are heroic military feats or the overcoming of extreme hardships or personal tragedies. Those things did happen, but not as often as reported by county histories).

For accounts on the Internet, if a source has not been cited, a discerning genealogist should contact the person who posted it. If the poster names a printed or primary source, that source should be checked. If the poster only says it was something an older family member told (or fails to identify any source) then it should be treated the same as an account from one's own older family members.

It Even Creeps into "Primary" Sources

Published county histories and accounts on the Internet are not the only sources of "written oral history." Some aspects of sources generally regarded as "primary" should also be viewed in that way. Perhaps the best such example is death certificates. Only certain items on them are truly "primary." The date and place of death of the decedent may be considered primary source information, because the death is the event that the certificate records. Other information on the certificates however – including that which is most useful to genealogists – cannot be regarded as "primary".

The death certificates of most states ask for the date and place of birth of the decedent and the names and birthplaces of the decedent's parents (including the mother's maiden name). When provided, they are a genealogical gold mine – but not one that can be automatically accepted without checking other sources. The person providing the information is unlikely to have been witness to the decedent's birth (unless the informant is a parent of the deceased, which is unusual). Most often, informants are spouses or children of the deceased and their memories of the names and birthplaces of the decedent's parents must be verified with other sources before being considered confirmed. The same questions must be asked about informants for death certificates that must be addressed in regard to those who tell life stories of their parents or grandparents to younger family members. Obituaries must be subjected to similar criteria if they give information on parents and more distant ancestors of the decedent.

Every Family Has Stories

Every family has unique stories, some accurate, some only partly accurate, and some entirely fictitious. Although each story is different, there are certain patterns that consistently emerge in family after family. Certain types of errors in oral traditions are found again and again. Genealogists should always be on the lookout for them and research primary sources to prove or disprove them because all are important to genealogists. In many cases, the same errors happen in different family stories for similar reasons. The following list includes some of the types of information provided in the various forms of oral history that most often turn out to be in error:

1. Ethnic Origins of Family Names
2. Maiden Names of Female Ancestors
3. Relationships to Someone Famous
4. Relationships to Royalty, Nobility, or Wealth
5. Birthplaces of Ancestors
6. Military Service of Ancestors
7. Two or More Brothers as Immigrants
8. Associations or Encounters With Famous People
9. Native American Ancestors

For all of these traditions, and many others, the information in oral history may be accurate or at least partially accurate. It should not be accepted as factual, however, until it can be verified with primary source material.

Chapter 2 - Ethnic Origins of Family Names

Among the first questions a beginning genealogist usually asks is "What country did the family come from?" or "What nationality is my name?" Though I did not begin actively researching my ancestry until my junior year in high school, I had been curious about it since very early childhood. I remember asking both of my parents what country their ancestors were from. My father said his ancestors were Dutch and my mother identified hers as Scotch-Irish. Well, neither of them was really wrong. I have Dutch ancestors on my father's side and I certainly have Scottish *and* Irish ancestors on my mother's side (though I am not entirely sure that the term *Scotch-Irish* is appropriate for any of them). But in terms of the surnames I was asking about (*Hite* in my father's case and *Williams* in my mother's case), both were wrong. My father's (and my) direct male line ancestors were German and my mother's direct male line ancestors were Welsh.

From *Deutsch* to *Dutch*

The erroneous assumption of the Dutch origin of my Hite ancestors is an easy one to explain, knowing what I know now. My father is a native of Kansas and his paternal ancestors participated in the gradual westward movement of the 19th century – coming to Kansas from Illinois in 1870, to Illinois from Ohio six years earlier and to Ohio from Pennsylvania in 1825 – Pennsylvania Dutch. The term *Pennsylvania Dutch* has confused genealogists and amateur historians for more than a century now. Many think it refers to people from the Netherlands who immigrated to Pennsylvania. In reality, the term *Pennsylvania Dutch* is properly *Pennsylvania Deutsch* or *Pennsylvania German* (*Deutsch* is the German word for *German* and *Deutschland* is the German word for *Germany*). The Pennsylvania Dutch are the descendants of the 17th and 18th century German immigrants that settled in Pennsylvania and my Hite (surname anglicized from *Heytt* or *Heyd*) ancestors were among them. In reality, there was very little settlement of true Dutch (Dutch from the Netherlands) in Pennsylvania during the colonial period.

Not to Mention Two World Wars

The Anglicization of the term *Deutsch* into *Dutch* is probably the single most common reason for the misperception that many descendants of German immigrants have that their ancestors were from the Netherlands. The reality of course is that the true Dutch from the Netherlands had virtually no role in the settlement of colonial Pennsylvania. Their efforts at settlement were concentrated in New York and the settlements they established there had already fallen into English hands by the time Pennsylvania was opened for settlement in the early 1680s. Despite this, the traditions continue. It is most common among descendants of colonial era German immigrants, but it can be found among the families of 19th century German immigrants also. The two world wars undoubtedly added to this misunderstanding because of the desire it created among many of German descent to disavow their origins. My father heard the story of our alleged Dutch origins from his own father, Oral Lee Hite, whom I never knew. It is likely that this misidentification resulted primarily from Oral's own misunderstanding of the term *Pennsylvania Dutch*. However, Oral also served in the United States Army during World War I. Therefore, I cannot rule out the possibility that he knew of his German heritage but was unwilling to admit it at the time. He would not have been alone in that.

Determining the ethnic identity of a surname is not always an easy task. However, the preceding example does show that one cannot automatically assume the origin given by older family members is correct. This is a situation that illustrates how important it is for genealogists to research and develop an understanding of, subjects related to genealogy. Studying the ethnic origins of specific types of surnames is certainly helpful, although only certain types of names clearly point to specific ethnic origins. Assigning specific ethnic identities to surnames is often risky business, especially in the case of families who have been in this country since the colonial era. Some are rather obvious – a name with the prefix "Mc" is undoubtedly Scottish or Irish and a name with the suffix "bach" or the anglicized version "baugh" as in Stambach or Stambaugh is obviously German. My own surname Hite, as it is currently spelled, however, is not one with an obvious ethnic identity. So other approaches were necessary.

Once the family had been traced to Pennsylvania in the colonial era, however, it was relatively easy to discount the Dutch origins. A little basic research into the history of the colonial era settlement of Pennsylvania demonstrates that Dutch immigration was not at all a significant factor. German immigration into Pennsylvania, however, had been heavy. Investigation of records in the county my family had been traced to (Bedford County) showed a strong German presence from the earliest days of settlement although there were also significant numbers of English and Scotch-Irish settlers there as well. The Dutch tradition in the family suggested German as the likely ethnic origin, but that alone was not proof. By that time, my father and I knew of another Hite family, that of Jost Hite of Virginia's Shenandoah Valley, that had documented evidence of its origins in the village of Bonfeld in the Kraichgau region of Germany. The spelling of that family's surname had originally been *Heyd* or *Heydt*. So by this time, even though we did not think we were related to the Shenandoah Valley Hite family (we now know we are not), we were leaning toward Germany as the country of origin of our Hite family. We were also aware, however, of an English Hight family that had been in New Jersey in the colonial era and some Revolutionary War pension applications we examined (specifically one for James Hite of Huntingdon County, Pennsylvania) gave us a clue that some of these English Hights may have migrated into central Pennsylvania (Huntingdon County is just northeast of Bedford County and was, in fact, formed from Bedford County in 1787). So we could not rule out England as our ancestral home either.

Consider the Neighbors – and the Given Names

In one respect, we were in the same situation in terms of ethnic identity as people with some of the most common English language surnames like Smith and Miller. Those names are often just that – English. But they can also be anglicized versions of the German names *Schmidt* and *Müller*, both of which actually mean the same thing in German. There are ways to look for clues about the ethnic origins of families when the surnames are ambiguous, especially in the colonial era. Researchers can look at tax

8

records or census records for the names of their ancestors' nearest neighbors. A Smith or Miller who was surrounded by neighbors with names like Stambach, Eberhardt, Zimmerman, and Eichelberger is obviously much more likely to be German than English. On the other hand, if a Smith was surrounded by Thompsons, Emerys, Shermans, and Pendletons, then it is most likely to be an English Smith – even if oral tradition identifies him as German. Another important clue in determining ethnic identity for colonial era families is the first names they used. Some like John and Mary do not tell researchers anything – they can be English or they can be the anglicized forms of Johannes and Maria. Others, though, seem to be more indicative of ethnic origin, particularly masculine given names. Some like Valentin, Joachim, Mathias, and Magdalena are a clear indication of German background, while Duncan and Hugh are almost entirely Scottish or Scotch-Irish. Robert can be found among English, Scots, and Scotch-Irish, but is almost never seen among Germans in the colonial era. Jacob can be English or German but is generally more common among Germans. Jonathan, Jeremiah, and Nathaniel seem to be almost entirely English.

Prior to the 1780s, the only Hite in the tax records of Bedford County was John Hite. His first name did not indicate anything and his nearest neighbors were ethnically mixed in origin. The surnames Ellinger, Funk and Nagel seemed obviously German, but others like Riley and Dougherty suggested that the bearers were of Irish origin. In the 1780s, two younger Hite men reached their majority – Christopher and Conrad Hite. The name *Christopher* also does not suggest a particular ethnic identity, but *Conrad* in that era hints strongly at German. Tax records gave further evidence for German origins by listing Christopher Hite as *Stophel* Hite (*Stophel* is a German nickname for Christopher). The final indication of German origins for the family, however, was two deeds of sale by John Hite. Though his surname was given as *Hite* throughout one of the documents (the other spelled it *Heit*), John's signature appeared at the end of both documents in German handwriting as *Johannes Heytt*. All of this evidence together was sufficient to prove that this family was of German origin. The most likely source of the mistaken Dutch tradition was the meaning of the term *Pennsylvania Dutch*, the term that has confused generations of genealogists and amateur historians. Proving the ethnic identity of a family name when it is not obvious from the name itself can be a painstaking process. It is, however, a critical part of genealogical research and it is not one for which family traditions can be accepted without documentation.

Right Name...Wrong Place

A misunderstanding of terminology is obviously one possible reason for an inaccurate identification of ethnic origins. There are, however, numerous other possibilities. An ethnic origin assigned to a particular surname might actually be that of another surname introduced into the lineage through female lines. My mother's understanding of Scotch-Irish origins for her Williams ancestors is probably explainable in this way. Her mother's maiden name was Grogan, obviously Irish in origin. My mother grew up in Black River Township of Cumberland County, North Carolina (as did I) and as far as she knew, her paternal ancestors could have been in that immediate vicinity from the time the area was first settled. The earliest European settlers of present-

9

day Black River Township had indeed been Scots – many of them Highlanders who had fled after the defeat of the forces of Bonnie Prince Charlie at the Battle of Culloden in 1746. It was these immigrants who established the Bluff Presbyterian Church in the township in 1758 – approximately four miles from my childhood home and the parent congregation of the Presbyterian Church my family attended. The church cemetery was filled with markers for people with names such as McNeil, McDonald, McCorquodale, Graham, and Bain – all obviously Scottish – and there was no reason for someone with no knowledge of surname ethnicity to assume that the Williams name was any different.

Names like Williams, however (patronymics with the possessive "s" at the end meaning "son of"), are generally of Welsh origin though some of the more common ones also developed independently in England. This fact is widely known by those who study origins of surnames in any depth at all, but it is not common knowledge among those who have not. I am sure that no one in my mother's family had researched this in any depth until her cousin, John C. Rosser, Jr., begin a detailed search for the family's origins after his retirement from the United States Army in the mid-1970s. Indeed, when I first decided to question him about my Williams roots, I learned there was a written single-paragraph autobiography in existence prepared about 1890 by my great-great-great-grandfather, John Carouth Williams (1808-1896). One of his statements in the account was quite specific about his Williams origins – "My great-grandfather, John Williams, came from Wales, a full blood Welshman." When one considers that John Carouth Williams never knew his great-grandfather (who died in 1783) or even his paternal grandfather (who died about 1799), his own account of his ancestors must be regarded as oral history as well, needing primary source verification. The statement that his great-grandfather came from Wales has yet to be proven or disproved. But the Welsh origins of the Williams surname are quite clear and there is no reason to assume that my Williams family is from a different country.

Rosser's extensive primary source research also demonstrated that the Williams family's residence in Black River Township only dated to 1850. The previous generations had lived along the border of the present-day townships of Dismal and Little Coharie in neighboring Sampson County since the colonial era. This area, about 30 miles from Black River Township, was not nearly as heavily Scottish in makeup as the later home of the Williams family. The family's neighbors there did include some Scots, but the earliest census records there also included numerous Welsh and English names, such as Howard, Phillips, Spell, and Butler. The neighboring families in this region, the home of the earliest members of this Williams family in southeastern North Carolina, are obviously a more important clue about their origins than their neighbors of a century later in Black River Township. They were not without Scottish connections, however. Other research did prove that John Carouth Williams was, through other lineages, of Scottish descent. His own middle name was the maiden name of his mother, Margaret (Carouth) Williams who had in fact been baptized at the Bluff Presbyterian Church in 1786. Margaret's father, Robert Carouth, was certainly of Scottish origin and very likely a native of Scotland. Her mother, Margaret (McFarland) Carouth, may also have been born in Scotland or she may have been the child of Scottish immigrants. So John Carouth Williams, though of Welsh descent in his direct male line, was at least half, and possibly as much as seven-eighths, of Scottish origin. Obviously, I have Scottish ancestors through my maternal grandfather. Equally obvious, however, is that to assign Scottish ethnicity to the Williams surname is incorrect. The Scottish ancestors of other surnames, combined with the heavily Scottish population in the immediate vicinity of my childhood home, were significant contributing factors in this erroneous assumption.

Surnames like Williams and McFarland, once one develops a rudimentary understanding of the distinctions between Welsh and Scottish family names, are fairly easy to identify and family traditions that incorrectly associate one of them with the wrong nationality can be disproved rather easily. As an example, it is not likely that the Scottish name *McDaniel* would have evolved into the Welsh *Daniels* in the American colonies (or vice versa) even though both names mean the same thing (son of Daniel). Other surnames, like my own surname *Hite*, are not so easy to place. Fortunately, my grandfather's misidentification of the family name as Dutch fell into a familiar pattern – the common fallacy that the term *Pennsylvania Dutch* refers to Dutch from the Netherlands rather than *Deutsch* (Germans) from Germany.

In the case of many surnames, determining the ethnic identity of the immigrants may follow logical patterns even if it is not easy. In the case of my Hite ancestors, their misidentification as Dutch fit the common pattern of the term *Pennsylvania Dutch* that refers to Germans. In the case of my maternal ancestors, their inaccurate designation as Scottish was rather easy to disprove by the fact that *Williams* is clearly identifiable as a Welsh, rather than a Scottish, surname. The source of the inaccuracy was an assignment of an ethnicity to them that actually belonged to the families of women they intermarried with.

Not all cases fit the obvious patterns, however. My aforementioned great-grandmother's maiden name – Bush – is another one like Smith and Miller that is often just what it appears to be – English. A number of Americans named Bush, however, are descendants of Germans whose surname was originally *Busch*. When I asked my grandmother about the ethnic origins of her mother's family, she had no hesitation in saying that they were Dutch – more specifically Pennsylvania Dutch. When I told her Pennsylvania Dutch actually meant German, she protested, "No, no, they were Pennsylvania Dutch *from* Holland." I said nothing and began searching for Germans in Pennsylvania whose name was originally *Busch* and even found a couple of German-born Revolutionary War soldiers with that name that seemed like likely candidates to be the father of my then earliest documented Bush ancestor, Joshua Bush. Then I checked for Joshua in the 1850 census for Pennsylvania. I found him in Columbus Township, Warren County, just as I expected. I did not know then that this county, in northwestern Pennsylvania, was not an area that had been settled by eighteenth-century German immigrants, the group I assumed I would find my Bush ancestors among. To my surprise, the census indicated that Joshua Bush (born about 1790) was a native of Connecticut, not Pennsylvania, as my grandmother and I had both assumed. At that point, I turned to the International Genealogical Index and found a Joshua Bush born 9 December 1789 in Enfield, Connecticut, son of Jonathan Bush and Patience Killam. This fit perfectly with my Joshua Bush's age (60) as given on the 1850 census. These given names did not sound very German or Dutch to me, but further research eventually convinced me that this was a valid record and that this Joshua was, indeed, my ancestor.

I was then able to follow the lineage back another three generations to an earlier Jonathan Bush, who was among the first settlers of Enfield when it was founded in 1683. It was soon quite clear to me from the family's long term residence in Enfield (a town founded primarily by settlers from northeastern Massachusetts, children of the Great Migration passengers of the 1630s) and the first names they used (the male line generations alternated between *Jonathan* and *Joshua* throughout the colonial era) that they were, to borrow a popular saying "as English as the Queen." Eventually, with the help of DNA testing, I determined that the earliest Jonathan Bush was a grandson of Reynold Bush, who had settled in what was then part of Cambridge, Massachusetts (present-day Newton Corners) by 1639. My grandmother had been wrong about the ethnic origins of her Bush ancestors, but not in the way that I had thought. Because she had identified them as *Pennsylvania* Dutch, I had assumed they were Germans like my Hite ancestors. Instead, they were New Englanders of English origin. How that had been transformed into Dutch was a mystery.

Another Ancestor was Dutch – Netherlands Dutch, not *Deutsch*

My research on other family lines eventually provided the answer. Lovisa Ingersoll (1792-1869), the wife of Joshua Bush, was born in Great Barrington, Massachusetts, a town located just a few miles east of the border with New York. Like nearly all Massachusetts towns, it was founded by the descendants of immigrants from England. In the century after the English conquest of New Netherland, however, some descendants of Dutch settlers who had lived in New York's Hudson River Valley began drifting the few miles eastward into western Massachusetts. Among them was Coenraet Hendrickse Borgaart (whose name was eventually spelled Conrad Burghardt) who settled in present-day Great Barrington in the 1730s. One of Conrad's granddaughters, Annatje Burghardt, married Oliver Ingersoll and anglicized her name as Hannah. They were the parents of Lovisa Ingersoll and through Lovisa, numerous Dutch names such as Huyck, Van Wie, Van Hoesen, and Van Valkenburgh were introduced into my lineage. My great-grandmother, Matilda Lovisa Bush, had been of Dutch (true Dutch, not Pennsylvania Dutch) descent after all. It was another case of an ethnicity being assigned to the wrong surname, just as it had happened in my mother's family. I had been hasty in my assumption that my grandmother had been referring to Pennsylvania Germans when she had said that her Bush ancestors had been Dutch. This is a prime example of the fact that there can be more than one plausible explanation for an error in assigning ethnicity. A discerning researcher must consider every conceivable possibility.

Hite and *Bush* are just two examples of surnames that are ethnically ambiguous. Some Americans with the Bush surname are descendants of English immigrants with the same spelling of the name. Others are descendants of Germans named *Busch* and a few may actually be Dutch, with ancestors whose surname was originally *Van den Bosch*. *Hite*, as it is spelled, may be a uniquely American name (although the spelling has been found in English records) but some are descendants of Germans surnamed Heidt, Heydt, or Heyd and others have English progenitors named Haight or Hight. One Hite family, concentrated in Union County, Kentucky, actually *is* Dutch in origin, having descended from three brothers with the surname *Heuts* who came to the United States as teenagers with Trappist monks in 1803. Obviously, to pigeonhole either of these names, as German, English, or Dutch, is a mistake – each family has to trace its own lineage to determine its ethnic origin. There are numerous other surnames, some of them quite common (such as Smith, Miller, and Brown) that are equally ambiguous in terms of nationality. However, when one person with a specific surname becomes particularly well known, it often happens that the ethnic origin of that person's family becomes the nationality that is forever associated with the surname in the popular imagination.

Same Name, *Not* Necessarily Same Nationality

This has happened with the Hite surname now to a large degree although my grandfather was evidently not aware of it, having assumed incorrectly that his Hite ancestors were Dutch. Most genealogists with connections to the Hite surname now assume that it is German if they have never heard otherwise. Often, it is (my own ancestors were Germans). The reason that it has been stereotyped as a German surname, however, is because of the fame of Jost Hite (1685-1761) who was prominent in the early settlement of the Shenandoah Valley of Virginia, arriving there in 1732 and becoming one of the largest landowners in the region. I am not related to Jost Hite and my estimate is that fewer than ten percent of all Americans with ancestors named Hite are related to him. Jost Hite's name is not one like George Washington or Thomas Jefferson that everyone knows. But all who research Hite genealogy learn of Jost Hite pretty quickly and unfortunately, many who learn of him jump to the conclusion that because he was German, their own Hite ancestors must also be German. In some families, the tradition is even more specific. Ever since I started researching my own ancestry in 1979, I have been meeting Hites who said that their ancestors were from the Alsace-Lorraine region along the border between Germany and France. The reason for this is obvious. A number of the histories of the Shenandoah Valley published in the late nineteenth and early twentieth centuries identified Jost Hite's European home as the Alsace-Lorraine. Often, they were as specific as saying that he was from the city of Strasbourg. In the 1970s, even that was disproved. Jost Hite was born Hans Justus Heyd in the village of Bonfeld in the Kraichgau region of Germany according to the church records there. Nonetheless, the tradition of origins in the Alsace-Lorraine continues to this day in many Hite families, some descendants of Jost Hite, and others not related to him at all. Even in families without a tradition that specific, the tradition of German origins is common, even for families of English origin.

Among the most obvious are the Hights of Virginia's eastern shore, some of whom may descend from John Hight, an Englishman who arrived in the area in 1656, more than half a century before Jost Hite arrived in the colonies in 1710. Some of this family drifted west into the south central and southwestern counties of Virginia and others moved further south into the Carolinas, Georgia, and Alabama. Some simplified their surname into *Hite* and others retained the *Hight* spelling. Even though these families did not settle in areas with a significant German population, the tradition of

German origins (even Alsatian origins) remains strong in many branches today. Jost Hite and his fame are the obvious reason for this. A similar tradition pervades the descendants of the colonial-era Hight family of central New Jersey that gave its name to the town of Hightstown. This family also appears to be of English origin. But despite this, some of their descendants have a tradition of German origins. The German tradition even extends to some Hiatt families (other spelling include Hyatt, Hiott, and Hiett). This is probably because there was a Quaker family named Hiatt in the Shenandoah Valley in the colonial era, living in the same vicinity as Jost Hite. This family's origins have also been documented in England. But again, despite this, the German tradition is strong in this family. Some material has even been posted on the Internet identifying an early member of this Hiatt family (John Hiatt, born 1674 in England) as a brother of Jost Hite who was born ten years later in Germany. Some websites even go as far as to say John Hiatt and Jost Hite were the same person! These websites list John Hiatt/Jost Hite as the same person and indicate that he had four wives (in reality, Jost Hite and John Hiatt each had two wives). Again, overeager researchers have identified their families as German because of Jost Hite and have not followed the path of documentation. I have yet to find any instance of the surname *Hiatt* (or any of its variations) evolving into *Hite* or any of its variations in any of my research. That should not be surprising given that *Hiatt* is obviously a two-syllable surname whereas *Hite* has only one syllable. Nonetheless, the traditions persist.

Obviously, determining the country of origin is one of the goals of most American genealogists. In some cases, the surname alone can demonstrate that or at least provide strong evidence for it. Other surnames are much more ethnically ambiguous, however, and require more research to link to a country across the Atlantic (for Americans of European origin). In these cases, one cannot take for granted that family traditions are accurate. Oral history must withstand the test of comparison to primary sources to be considered proven.

Chapter 3 - Maiden Names of Female Ancestors

There is a survey I have wanted to take for years. I have always wished I could just call people randomly or stop people on the street and ask them to tell me the maiden names of their grandmothers. I really wonder how many people could give an answer. Then I would like to have some means of verifying the information given to me by the ones who said they did know. My guess is that the percentage that said they knew AND got it right would actually be pretty low. I think it's safe to say that most people know the maiden names of their mothers, even though that, like anything else, should be backed up with documentation. But oral traditions about the maiden names of grandmothers and any female ancestors further back must be documented before they can be accepted as factual.

One has to ask several key questions when considering the accuracy of the information about female ancestors' maiden names provided by living relatives:

1. Did the informant know his or her grandmother or great-grandmother?
2. If so, how old was the informant when the grandmother or great-grandmother died?
3. If the informant knew the grandmother, did he or she live in close proximity to her?
4. Did the informant live in the same area where the grandmother grew up?

The Married Name of an Aunt?

Obviously, if the informants knew their grandmothers well, the chances are better that they knew their maiden names. But even then, there are potential pitfalls. There is always the chance that a surname someone remembers might turn out to be the married name of a grandmother's sister or some other name that was somehow connected with the family (for example, the surname of a cousin known to be related through the grandmother in question). In my own case, I asked both grandmothers about their families when I first became interested in genealogy (my grandfathers were already dead). Both of them DID know the maiden names of the grandmothers although each of them gave me a slightly less than perfect spelling for one of the two and one of the misspellings ultimately resulted in my pursuing false leads for several years (note the Hambleton/Hamilton confusion in a previous chapter). My paternal grandmother actually had the names of all of her great-grandparents, including maiden names of great-grandmothers (this was the result of a school project she had done when she was ten years old). She had not known her great-grandparents but she had been able to ask her parents (and one grandmother) about this. As it turned about, she only had the maiden names of two of the four great-grandmothers right. In both cases, the incorrect surnames she had given me were actually the surnames of men who had married into the families of the great-grandfathers involved. She had given the name of her paternal great grandmother, Phally Bagley (1789-1845) as Tewksbury.[2] In searching the International

---

[2] As mentioned earlier, my grandmother had given the maiden name of a maternal great-grandmother as Abbey, when it was actually Sherman. The surname Abbey had come from the husband of a sister of her

Genealogical Index (once a more dependable source than it is now) for Phally and her husband Jesse Bagley, I found the marriage of Jesse Bagley and Phally *Saunders* in 1808 in Susquehanna County, Pennsylvania. When I mentioned that to her, she recalled that her uncle, John Lincoln Bagley, had disagreed with the person who gave her Tewksbury as Phally's maiden name when she worked on the project. John had believed Phally to be a Saunders.

My research eventually proved that Saunders was the correct maiden name for Phally Bagley, who was born in 1789 in Charlestown, Rhode Island. I eventually traced her lineage to Tobias Saunders, an early settler of Westerly, Rhode Island who died there in 1695. The Tewksbury surname, it turned out, was the name of a man who married into the Bagley family prior to their arrival in Susquehanna County. The Tewksbury and Bagley families were both descendants of early settlers of Amesbury, Massachusetts and the Bagleys had been joined by some of their Tewksbury relatives in their migration path from Amesbury to Weare, New Hampshire (where Jesse Bagley was born in 1786), then to Hartland, Vermont and finally to Susquehanna County in 1804.

Phally (Saunders) Bagley was the only one of my grandmother's paternal great-grandparents that she did not correctly identify. Given that Phally died in 1845 that is not surprising. Phally was the only grandparent that her father, Horace Dever Bagley and his brother John had not known personally. They also had only vague memories of their father, John Webster Bagley, who died in the Civil War. Their other grandmother, Eliza Ann (Nash) Babcock had lived until at least 1870 and they had both known her. It is no accident that Grandma had identified her correctly but had misidentified Phally.

There are more famous cases of incorrect maiden names that have led numerous researchers astray for years. Perhaps one of the best-known cases is one that was resolved only recently, the maiden name of Eve Earnest of Bedford County, Pennsylvania, better known as "Indian Eve." The reason that she is known by that name is that she lived as a Native American captive for several years during the American Revolution after Native Americans attacked her home and killed her husband, Adam Earnest (or Ernst). For the past forty years, it has been printed and reprinted in numerous publications that her maiden name was Imler, which also happens to be a very prominent name in Bedford County (there are two small towns in the county named for them, Imler and Imlertown). For years, the numerous Imler descendants in Bedford County have proudly claimed her as a distant aunt, identifying her as a sister of their ancestor, Georg Michael Imler.

No Male Relatives to "Claim" Her

Later research, however, uncovered documentation that tells a far different story. Records of the German pastor, Henry Melchior Muhlenberg, reveal the marriage of Adam Ernst and Eva Catharina Hillebart, daughter of Adam Hillebart in Augustus

---

great-grandfather, Joshua Bush – ironically, not the husband of Matilda. Grandma did have memories of a Bush-Ingersoll-Abbey reunion involving her family and may have just assumed Abbey was an ancestral name that fit in somewhere.

Lutheran Church in or near New Hanover, Pennsylvania on 28 November 1757. A few years later (3 April 1762), this couple had a son, Georg Adam Ernst, baptized in Tinicum Lutheran Church in the same vicinity, with Eva's brother, Georg Adam Hillebart (spelled Hellepart in the record) as a witness. This date on this baptismal record matches perfectly with the birthdate inferred from the age and death date given on the tombstone of Georg Adam Earnest in Bedford County, who is known to be Indian Eve's son. A 1773 deed in Bucks County, Pennsylvania, reveals the sale of the farm owned by Adam Ernst and this is shortly before he began appearing on tax records in Bedford County. The case made by the documentation is clear-cut here. The maiden name of "Indian Eve" Earnest (or Ernst) was Hillebart, not Imler. Most of her father's male line descendants spell the name as *Hillpot* today. It is also noteworthy that none of Eve's brothers or any other Hillpot relatives accompanied her and her husband to Bedford County, so Hillpot is not a Bedford County surname. There have never been any Hillpots there to "claim" Indian Eve as one of their own, even though she was, so until more careful researchers entered the picture, the Imlers' claim to her was largely uncontested, even though it was not supported by any documentary evidence. It is true that there were quite a few intermarriages in later generations between the Earnest and Imler families, so it would not be surprising if an Earnest, who was in fact also a descendant of the Imlers, concluded that his or her Imler link was through the wrong ancestor. Given Indian Eve's fame, it is not surprising that the many Imlers in the area would be happy to claim her as theirs and with none of her real birth family there to counter the claim, it was uncontested. Nonetheless, no discerning genealogist will accept a lineage based on a claim that is not supported by evidence in primary sources.

The Name May be in Your Lineage – Just Somewhere Else

An even more famous case of a misidentified wife was Anna Maria, the first wife of Jost Hite (1685-1761) of the Shenandoah Valley and the mother of his children. Numerous histories of specific Shenandoah Valley counties were published in the late nineteenth and early twentieth centuries that identified her as Anna Maria Dubois, a member of a wealthy Huguenot family. This identification was accepted unquestioningly by most of Jost Hite's descendants until the late 1970s when documentation proving otherwise was uncovered in Germany. The church records of Jost's native village (Bonfeld in the Kraichgau region) listed the marriage on 11 November 1704 of "Johan Justus Heyd, linenweaver and son of Johannis Heyd – butcher and civic councilor here" to Anna Maria Merckle, daughter of Abraham Merckle who was also a citizen of Bonfeld. This revelation came as a shock to many of Jost Hite's descendants and some of them refuse to accept the validity of it to this day. However, the reason for the misidentification becomes obvious when examining the backgrounds of the spouses of Jost's children. The fact is that three of Jost Hite's sons married granddaughters of Sarah Dubois Vanmeter and her husband Joost Vanmeter who lived in the same area of Kingston, New York where Jost lived when he first arrived in the colonies. Descendants of Joost and Sarah had also moved south, settling in Frederick County, Maryland. Descendants of the three sons of Jost (John, Isaac, and Abraham Hite) who married Dubois descendants obviously made the mistake of assigning the wrong maiden name to the wrong female ancestor – another manifestation of a common problem in genealogy.

This error found its way into print and became a tradition for all of Jost Hite's descendants – even though it was only the descendants of the aforementioned three sons who had a connection to a family named Dubois.

When Middle Names are Not "Family" Names

Erroneous assumptions about mothers' maiden names can also result from middle names that were obviously surnames. A descendant of someone named James Madison Smith might easily jump to the conclusion that the ancestor's mother was a Madison – perhaps even a relative of the President of that name. It is here that a lack of knowledge about nineteenth century naming customs can lead overeager genealogists astray. It was common in the United States throughout the nineteenth century and even into the early twentieth century to name children – particularly boys – after Presidents or other admired public figures. In particular, genealogists can expect to find a large number of men named for a President during the years he campaigned or was in office – a number named James Madison were born between 1809 and 1817, for example. Such names were not always those of nationally known public figures either. They can easily be the names of Congressional representatives from the area of someone's birth. Another common source of middle names in the late nineteenth and early twentieth centuries was the surnames of attending physicians. While it is true that family surnames were often used as middle names for children, genealogists must take care not to jump to the conclusion that this was always the case. A surname as a middle name is a clue about a connection to a family of that name – not proof. Research on a surname used as a middle name for a child might reveal that there was a local politician or doctor by that name. When that does prove to be the case, a discerning genealogist must consider the possibility that the name was not chosen because of a genetic connection.

Death Certificates Can Be Wrong

These inaccurate maiden names, whatever their origins, can sometimes find their way into records that are considered primary sources. One of the most common sources for the maiden names of female ancestors is a death certificate of one of their children. In most states, these death certificates include a slot for the maiden name of the mother of the deceased. When a researcher obtains a certificate with a maiden name for a mother that was previously known only by her first name, it is a major breakthrough. After all, finding the maiden names of female ancestors is often one of the most difficult challenges genealogists face. However, as discerning genealogists know, death certificates cannot be considered primary sources for information concerning a decedent's birth – they are only primary sources for the decedent's death because they are created at the time of death. The date of death, place of death, and place of burial are all usually noted on death certificates and the certificate is a primary source for that information. However, data provided about the decedent's birth – date of birth, place of birth, and names of parents – must be considered secondary information because the record was not created at the time of birth, except in the case of stillborn infants.

This does not mean that researchers should ignore mothers' maiden names that appear on death certificates – far from it. What it means is that researchers should immediately begin checking for wills, estates, and deeds in the appropriate areas for people with the maiden name found on the certificate. Very often, such a document will be found that identifies the mother of the decedent as an heir of someone with the same surname a generation before, thus proving the accuracy of the surname on the death certificate. But what if no such proof is found? What if no one of the maiden name given on the death certificate appears in the appropriate area? Researchers then have to consider the possibility that the informant for the death certificate reported the maiden name of the decedent's mother inaccurately.

Who Was the Informant?

To determine the likelihood of an inaccurately reported maiden name for a decedent's mother, one should determine the relationship of the informant to the deceased. For people who married and had children, the informant is most likely to be the spouse or one of the children. Researchers should determine whether or not the informant knew the mother of the deceased and if so, how well. A maiden name for a grandmother who died before the informant was born is much more questionable than the maiden name of a grandmother who lived until the informant was in his or her teens or twenties. It is also worthwhile to know if the informant lived in proximity to the grandmother in question.

Expand the Search

If further research reveals that a maiden name for the mother of a decedent cited on a death certificate is questionable, then it is worthwhile to obtain a death certificate for a sibling of the deceased. If the mother's maiden name is the same on a sibling's death certificate, the credibility of it is strengthened (unless the informant is the same person in both cases, which is unlikely). Often, the most credible of death certificates are those of people who died childless. In those cases, it is not at all unusual for a sibling of the deceased to be the informant for a death certificate. Assuming the siblings were full siblings, the informant would have had the same mother as the deceased. Therefore, the odds that the maiden name given for the mother of the deceased is correct are very high.

A death certificate led me astray for several years for one of my own lineages. One of my great-great-grandmothers was Mary Etta (Bolling) Stewart who died about 1890 in Rockingham County, North Carolina. That date of death is too early for a death certificate in North Carolina. Her granddaughter, Melba (Grogan) Williams (my grandmother) was not born until 1909 and therefore did not know her grandmother – in fact she had no actual memory of any of her grandparents and only one lived into her lifetime. She did, however, remember a brother of Mary Etta – Charles Bolling who, she recalled, visited a few times when she was a child. Even better, she knew where Charles had lived – Winston-Salem, North Carolina. Although she did not know his date of death, having had no further contact with him as an adult, I was confident that I could obtain a death certificate for him based on what I already knew.

Did my Grandmother Date Her Cousin?

I was right. I ordered a death certificate and when it arrived, the names of both parents were entered in the appropriate slots – William Bolling and Sarah Angel. I had found another set of great-great-great-grandparents. The name Angel was familiar to me – my grandmother, as a teenager, had dated a boy named Lyman Angel. I wondered if she had unknowingly dated a cousin.

I was in college at the time so a couple of years passed before I had a chance to research this family further. When I located them on the 1870 census of Rockingham County, I was a bit surprised. William Bolling (listed only by the initials W.S.) was there, aged 45, which was about the age I had expected him to be (Mary Etta, recently married and living next door, was 17 and Charles was ten). William's wife, however, was not named Sarah. Instead, her name was Elizabeth and, like him, she was aged 45.

I thought little of this at first. By 1870, Charles Bolling was ten years old with two younger siblings and I found it easy to believe that his mother Sarah had died giving birth to him or one of the later children and that William had remarried. It *was* a bit puzzling that William's presumed second wife Elizabeth (who, if she was not Charles's mother, must have been in at least her mid-thirties by the time she married William) had no children by a previous marriage (there were no children of another surname in the household which one would assume would have been brought in by a remarried widow). Still, the idea that Elizabeth was the stepmother of Charles (and also Mary Etta) seemed the most logical conclusion at that point.

Marriage Records Trump Death Certificates

I felt fortunate that William Bolling (and presumably his first wife) had both been born in Virginia rather than North Carolina and started their married life there (the two oldest children in the household, along with the recently-wed Mary Etta, had been born in Virginia but the three younger ones were born in North Carolina). Marriage records are easier to find in Virginia. I checked the Virginia counties that bordered Rockingham County first and struck paydirt in the first county I examined – Pittsylvania County, Virginia. This item threw me a curveball though. I found a marriage record that indicated William S. Bowling married Elizabeth Martin - not Sarah Angel - on 15 October 1846.

At first I thought this might be the wrong William Bolling. The difference in the spelling of the surname did not faze me because I knew enough by that time to be aware that the spelling of surnames could vary in that era. As I thought about it though, I became more convinced this was the correct William. The middle initial matched the 1870 census listing, he was married to an Elizabeth, and the one listed in the 1870 census would have been about 21 in 1846 – a likely age to marry. Perhaps my ancestor's name was Elizabeth Martin, rather than Sarah Angel.

20

The next step was the 1850 census. I found a couple named William and Elizabeth Boling, both aged 24, in Pulaski County, Virginia. It was immediately apparent that this was the same couple that had married in Pittsylvania County in 1846. A household headed by Bailey Martin, aged 66, was just five pages away and the marriage record had identified him as the father of Elizabeth Martin. The couple had two young children, George W. Boling (aged 2) and Sarah E. Boling (aged 1).

This listing did not prove or disprove that this William and Elizabeth were the same ones listed in Rockingham County, North Carolina in 1870. The ages fit, but the oldest child with William and Elizabeth in 1870 was an 18-year old James W. Bolling – not born yet in 1850. If this was the same couple, their oldest two children were no longer at home in 1870 – which would not be surprising. Nonetheless it was clear that only the 1860 census could answer the question. Their relocation to Pulaski County, three counties west of Pittsylvania County, raised doubts in my mind. I had checked Pittsylvania County because it bordered Rockingham County, North Carolina. But Pulaski County was a much greater distance away.

Follow the Trail to its End

Obviously, the only way to come up with a definitive answer was to locate William Bolling on the 1860 census. There were children who were teenagers in the 1870 census who were sure to be in the 1860 household. The household turned up that year in Surry County, North Carolina – west of Rockingham County separated from it by Stokes County. In the household were William and Elizabeth Bolling, both aged 35 (compatible with the 1850 Pulaski County household *and* the 1870 Rockingham County family). A male named G.W. Bolling, aged 13 was there, along with Sarah E. Bolling, aged 11 – proving beyond doubt that this was the same family listed in 1850 in Pulaski County. Also in the household were a male named J.W. Bolling, aged 9 (compatible with James W. Bolling, aged 18 in the Rockingham County listing of 1870), a female named M.E. Bolling, aged 7 (obviously my great-great-grandmother Mary Etta, aged 17 and married by 1870) and a male named C.W., aged 1 (obviously Charles, aged 10 in 1870, whose full name I knew as Charles Welborn Bolling). There was one discrepancy – a male J.M. Bolling, aged 5 in 1860, appears identical with a Josephine Bolling, aged 15 in 1870. That was probably an error in the gender column by the 1860 census taker – the rest of the household is too similar to the 1870 listing in Rockingham County to reach any conclusion other than the family being the same.

With that, all doubt was removed – my great-great-great-grandmother Bolling was Elizabeth Martin, *not* Sarah Angel. So how had she been so badly misnamed? Another look at the death certificate of Charles Welborn Bolling revealed that the informant was a *Mrs.* W.W. Bolling. A bit of further research indicated that this informant was a daughter-in-law of Charles – one who probably never knew his mother Elizabeth, who apparently died before 1900. A daughter-in-law of a decedent is certainly less likely to know the maiden name of a decedent's mother than a child of the decedent is. Mrs. W.W. Bolling may very well have provided information for Charles's obituary too – it also gives his mother's name as Sarah Angel.

Figure 1 - This death certificate for Charles Welborn Bolling (1859-1949) gives the maiden name of his mother as Sarah Angel. However the marriage record of his parents and subsequent census records prove beyond question that his mother's name was actually Elizabeth Martin.

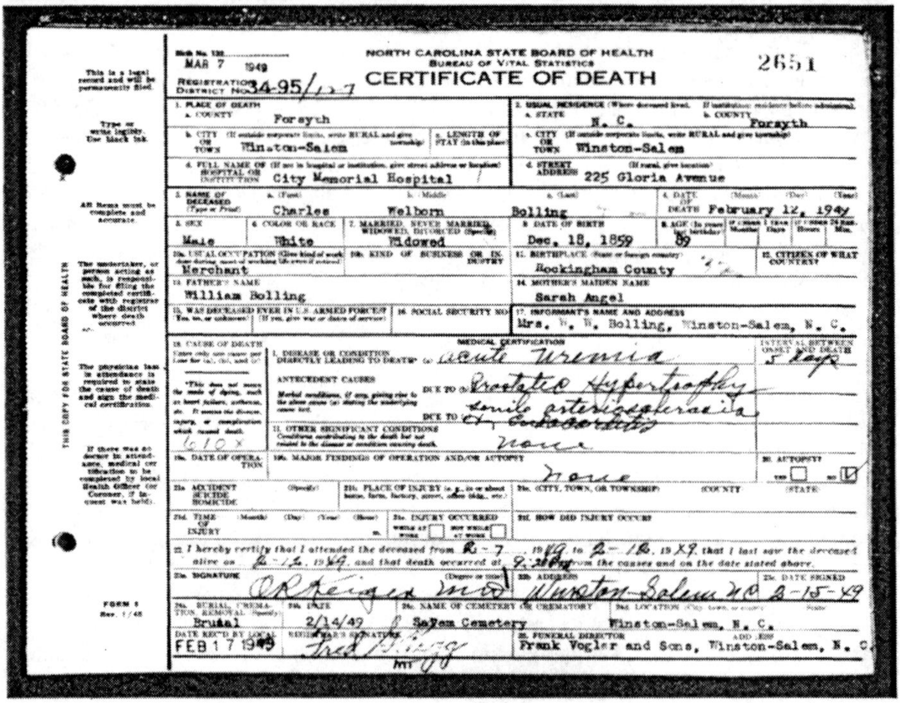

MAR 7 1949

REGISTRATION DISTRICT NO. 34-95/127

NORTH CAROLINA STATE BOARD OF HEALTH
BUREAU OF VITAL STATISTICS

CERTIFICATE OF DEATH

2651

1. PLACE OF DEATH
a. COUNTY Forsyth
b. CITY OR TOWN Winston-Salem
d. FULL NAME OF HOSPITAL OR INSTITUTION City Memorial Hospital

2. USUAL RESIDENCE
a. STATE N. C. b. COUNTY Forsyth
c. CITY OR TOWN Winston-Salem
d. STREET ADDRESS 225 Gloria Avenue

3. NAME OF DECEASED (Type or Print) a. (First) Charles b. (Middle) Welborn c. (Last) Bolling
4. DATE OF DEATH February 12, 1949
5. SEX Male
6. COLOR OR RACE White
7. MARRIED, NEVER MARRIED, WIDOWED, DIVORCED (Specify) Widowed
8. DATE OF BIRTH Dec. 18, 1859
9. AGE 89
10a. USUAL OCCUPATION Merchant
10b. KIND OF BUSINESS OR INDUSTRY
11. BIRTHPLACE Rockingham County
12. CITIZEN OF WHAT COUNTRY?
13. FATHER'S NAME William Bolling
14. MOTHER'S MAIDEN NAME Sarah Angel
15. WAS DECEASED EVER IN U.S. ARMED FORCES?
16. SOCIAL SECURITY NO.
17. INFORMANT'S NAME AND ADDRESS Mrs. W. W. Bolling, Winston-Salem, N. C.

MEDICAL CERTIFICATION

18. CAUSE OF DEATH
I. DISEASE OR CONDITION DIRECTLY LEADING TO DEATH (a) acute uremia — INTERVAL BETWEEN ONSET AND DEATH 5 days
ANTECEDENT CAUSES
DUE TO (b) Prostatic Hypertrophy
DUE TO (c) senile arteriosclerosis
II. OTHER SIGNIFICANT CONDITIONS None
610 X
19a. DATE OF OPERATION
19b. MAJOR FINDINGS OF OPERATION AND/OR AUTOPSY None
20. AUTOPSY? Yes ☐ No ☑
21a. ACCIDENT SUICIDE HOMICIDE (Specify)
21b. PLACE OF INJURY
21c. (CITY, TOWN, OR TOWNSHIP) (COUNTY) (STATE)
21d. TIME OF INJURY
21e. INJURY OCCURRED WHILE AT WORK ☐ NOT WHILE AT WORK ☐
21f. HOW DID INJURY OCCUR?

22. I hereby certify that I attended the deceased from 2-7, 1949 to 2-12, 1949, that I last saw the deceased alive on 2-12, 1949, and that death occurred at 9:20 from the causes and on the date stated above.
23a. SIGNATURE O R Keiger MD
23b. ADDRESS Winston-Salem NC
23c. DATE SIGNED 2-15-49
24a. BURIAL, CREMATION, REMOVAL (Specify) Burial
24b. DATE 2/14/49
24c. NAME OF CEMETERY OR CREMATORY Salem Cemetery
24d. LOCATION Winston-Salem, N. C.
DATE REC'D BY LOCAL REGISTRAR FEB 17 1949
REGISTRAR'S SIGNATURE Fred [illegible]
25. FUNERAL DIRECTOR Frank Vogler and Sons, Winston-Salem, N. C.

It May be the Wrong Grandmother

So where did the surname *Angel* come into the picture? Or for that matter, what about the first name *Sarah*? William and Elizabeth (Martin) Bolling were still alive at the time of the 1880 census and that one listed Elizabeth as Elizabeth S. Bolling – so perhaps her middle name was Sarah. But the surname *Angel* has another history. As it turned out, the mother of Charles Welborn Bolling's wife (Mary Maranda Webster) was Rebecca Angel. Mrs. W.W. Bolling had simply confused the maiden names of her husband's grandmothers. Mary Maranda Webster Bolling was not genetically related to me, so I have no connection to the Angel family. I was able to turn my attention to the Martin family and soon learned that Elizabeth's father, Bailey Martin, was a son of a Revolutionary War soldier named George Martin (1752-1805) and his wife Mary Bailey, who was still alive in 1841. George was a native of Fairfax County, in northern Virginia, and Mary was from neighboring Loudoun County, a daughter of Joseph Bailey. Ironically, Fairfax County is also where I was born – Fort Belvoir, to be more precise.

As my search for Mary Etta Bolling's mother proved, even a death certificate can lead one astray. Had I accepted the information on Charles Bolling's death certificate, I might still be looking for a nonexistent female ancestor named Sarah Angel to this day. As it is, I have identified my ancestor Elizabeth Martin, her parents, and her paternal grandparents – all with *true* primary sources.

Obviously, discovering maiden names for female ancestors is an important goal in genealogy. It is a challenging process, but also a very rewarding one, as my Martin research has shown. In order to avoid following false leads, genealogists should take care to properly verify any maiden names given to them verbally by other family members or written from memory. The further back the female ancestor in question is, the greater the need is for verification. Older relatives' memories, published county histories, and even maiden names of mothers given on death certificates all demand further verification.

Chapter 4 - Relationships to Someone Famous

This is one thing that genealogists must learn to take for granted. When one researches a surname that also happens to be the surname of someone famous, regardless of how common a surname it is, somebody, somewhere, will have claimed to be related to the famous person. The tradition will have been passed down verbally and perhaps even have been written somewhere. If a researcher's own surname, or the maiden name of a mother or grandmother was something like Washington, Lincoln, Jefferson, Boone, or Franklin, just to name a few, the tradition will be there. There is, of course, a chance that the tradition is true. The mistake a lot of genealogists make in those cases is to focus all of their research on the families of the famous people and not consider any other possibilities. Genealogists who pick someone of an appropriate surname in the past and only try to trace that person's descendants down to find a link to their earliest documented ancestors usually find only frustration. One thing to keep in mind if one is researching the surname of someone famous is that in most cases, if there is a link to that person, it is usually not that difficult to find. The families of the famous have usually been researched more extensively than other families and often (though not always), the famous are connected to particularly affluent families that left a lot of records. So chances are, if one does not find a link to the famous person relatively quickly, the link is not there. Some examples can be dismissed outright. I once saw something in a published genealogy that mentioned a woman with the Lincoln surname who had married into the family that was the focus of the book. The author did not give the names of the woman's parents, but she did state that the Lincoln bride was a "daughter of a brother of President Lincoln." Well, anyone who knows anything at all about Lincoln's childhood knows that his only brother died in infancy, so that claim can be dismissed without a second thought. Even if Abraham Lincoln did have brothers, the claim would have to be regarded with suspicion, because the author did not provide the name of the bride's father. That, in and of itself, shows a lack of primary source research. Chances are a careful researcher will not know the name of an ancestor's uncle without knowing the name of the parent that the uncle was a brother to.

Were They Neighbors?

In terms of a possibility of a relationship to a famous person, the major question to be considered is this – "Based on what I have documented about my ancestors, is this relationship feasible?" Suppose a researcher's surname is Jefferson. Somewhere, sometime, s/he will have undoubtedly been told that s/he was related to Thomas Jefferson. But suppose the earliest confirmed Jefferson ancestor is documented as having been born in upstate New York in the early 19th century? The chances of such a person being related to Thomas Jefferson are virtually nonexistent. If one studies typical migration patterns in America during the colonial and antebellum eras, one would find that relocation from Virginia to upstate New York was virtually unheard of. On the other hand, if the earliest documented Jefferson ancestor was born about that same time in Kentucky, then the odds are more in favor of a relationship to Jefferson, because there was a great deal of migration from Virginia to Kentucky. One must also look at the economic circumstances of their ancestors when considering this possibility. Not all of

Thomas Jefferson's relatives were affluent, but it is not likely that many of them were among the impoverished of the antebellum period. If a Jefferson ancestor in Kentucky never owned land, the likelihood of a relationship to the author of the Declaration of Independence is reduced dramatically.

DNA Can Prove or Disprove It

Modern technology has provided new means of establishing male line relationships through testing of men's Y-chromosomes. If one researches the subject on the Internet, one will find links to websites describing thousands of these single-surname projects that are going on today. At least two that have revealed significant information involve the surnames of famous people – Daniel Boone and Abraham Lincoln.

Seventeen documented male-line relatives of Daniel Boone had participated in the Boone DNA study as of 2012 – some of them direct descendants of Daniel, and others descendants of his brothers, uncles, and cousins. The Y-chromosomes of all seventeen men matched closely, as expected. Six other Boone men, who had not traced their ancestry back definitively far enough to prove or disprove a relationship to Daniel, also matched this DNA reading, proving that they are somehow related. But their Y-chromosomes do not match those of any of the other participating Boones. In fact, at least sixteen separate Boone families have been identified by this study, none of them related to each other in the male line. It is obvious from these results that not all Boones have a common European ancestor in the male line and certainly, not all are related to Daniel Boone – even though it is likely that many, probably most, of them grew up with an understanding that they were.

Proximity: Clue, Not Proof

In the case of the Lincoln surname study, six known relatives of the Great Emancipator (descendants of Samuel Lincoln, Abraham's immigrant ancestor) have participated in the test as of 2010. As one would expect, they all match each other closely. Five other Lincolns, however, also came to New England in the seventeenth century and ironically, all of them settled (temporarily or permanently) in Hingham, Massachusetts, the same town that Samuel Lincoln established as his permanent residence. A logical conclusion for any genealogist to reach is that these six immigrants were all part of the same extended family in England. DNA test results on descendants of four of the others, however, show that not only were none of these other immigrants related to Samuel Lincoln, only two of the other four were related to each other! Four separate Lincoln families came to Massachusetts in the 1630s and all of them established some sort of tie to the town of Hingham. This is a very surprising result, given that Lincoln is not a particularly common name. For four unrelated Smiths to settle in the same town would not be so surprising. This example not only illustrates that no discerning researcher can assume a relationship to a famous person with the same surname, but it also demonstrates that the same surname in the same area does not prove kinship. The odds against four unrelated Lincolns settling in, or passing through, the same Massachusetts town in the seventeenth century seems extraordinary. Yet it happened. Undoubtedly, many descendants of these other Lincoln immigrants have grown up with an understanding of a relationship to Abraham Lincoln and if they succeeded in tracing their lineages to ancestors from Hingham, Massachusetts, they were probably confident that the tradition was correct. However, as DNA has shown, if they traced to an immigrant in Hingham other than Samuel Lincoln, the tradition was wrong.

The likely origin of the Lincoln surname may help explain the oddity of several unrelated immigrants named Lincoln settling in Hingham around the same time. The surname apparently refers to the English town of Lincoln, which derives its name from the term "lake colony". It is possible that when people first began taking surnames in that region, several men who were unrelated (at least in the direct male line) may have adopted the Lincoln surname because of their residence in the town of Lincoln or a similar association to the "lake colony". If descendants of all of these men remained in the region for several centuries, it is not at all surprising that descendants of all of them that chose to sail to New England would have established residence in proximity to each other upon arrival there. These immigrants may have been former neighbors in England who only coincidentally shared a surname.

Famous on a Smaller Scale

Names such as Daniel Boone and Abraham Lincoln are known to nearly all Americans. Other people, who were famous at one time in a specific area, are not so widely known. In these cases, however, anyone with the surnames of those people learns of them quickly when beginning work on genealogy, especially in this day of the Internet. Jost Hite, already discussed at length previously, is one such example. Anyone who begins work on Hite genealogy learns of him pretty quickly. My father and I certainly did when we began work on our own genealogy in the summer of 1979. It did not take long, though, for us to figure out that we were almost certainly not descendants of Jost and we gradually came to believe that we were not related to him at all. Our family, unlike many other Hites, had no connection whatsoever to the Shenandoah Valley. Most other Hites we encountered remained convinced that even if they were not direct descendants of Jost Hite, they must have a common ancestor in Germany. This was particularly true for those who could trace their families to the Shenandoah Valley.

Once again, DNA testing provided the answers. A Hite-Hoyt surname project was launched for men with the Hite and Hoyt surnames, along with many other spellings both German and English. To this point, no fewer than 23 separate families have been identified, including thirteen who spell the surname as *Hite* (at least in part, some extended families have varied spellings for different branches). Four direct male-line descendants of Jost Hite took the DNA test and, as expected, all of them matched each other closely. No other Hite has matched the DNA reading of Jost's family, however, proving that not only are they not descendants of Jost, they do not (as many thought) share a common ancestor with him in Germany. No fewer than eight separate Hite lineages can be found in the Shenandoah Valley – a situation similar to the separate Lincoln families in Hingham, Massachusetts. Some rational thought on the matter leads to the reason for this in the case of the Hite surname.

Jost Hite's original name, as recorded in Germany, was Hans Justus Heyd. The surname Heyd has many variations in 17th and 18th century Germany records (Heydt, Heid, Heidt, Hayd, and Haydt). The most common Germany spelling of this name today is *Heidt* and though it is not one of the most common German surnames (in no way comparable to *Schmidt* or *Müller*), it is by no means rare. No fewer than twenty-three German men with one of the aforementioned variations of the surname can be documented as having arrived in the American colonies in the 18th century and there may have been others that have not yet been located in existing records. Hans Justus Heyd was one of the first (he arrived in 1710) and his surname underwent a few changes before it became established as *Hite* in the Shenandoah Valley, where he rose to prominence after his arrival in 1732. The Shenandoah Valley, as it prospered, drew large numbers of German settlers. It is easy to understand why those with the surname Heyd (or one of the other variations) would have seen it evolve into Hite – that had become the accepted spelling in the Shenandoah Valley. The name could just as easily have evolved into Hyde – and often did in Pennsylvania (the letters "d" and "t" sound much more similar in German than in English). The spelling of my own family's surname became *Hite* in Bedford County, Pennsylvania, even though there were relatives further east (in Berks County, Pennsylvania) who retained the German spelling *Heydt*. At the time my ancestors settled in Bedford County, it was one of the westernmost frontiers of the American colonies and education was by no means readily available. Ironically, the family of Jost Hite may have influenced the spelling of my own family's name. Two of Jost's sons, Jacob and Abraham Hite, made efforts to obtain land in the county just after its formation in 1771. This sparked a case that reached the county courts and my immigrant ancestor (referred to as John *Hight* in the court record) served on the second Grand Jury convened in the new county. It was about this time that the county's tax collectors began spelling his surname as *Hite* for the first time – the tax records in the parent county of Cumberland had always listed him as *Hight* or *Height*. Jost Hite's sons may have influenced the spelling of my family's surname, even though they were not related to my ancestors.

They Were Rich – We Were Poor

Even without the proof that DNA testing provided, my family had ample reason to believe there was no connection to Jost Hite. In the latter half of the 18th century, they lived in Bedford County, Pennsylvania, not overly distant from the Shenandoah Valley (maybe ninety miles) but one would think that if they were related to Jost, who had established himself as such a prominent citizen in the Valley, they would have located there. My ancestors were also among the poorest residents of Bedford County, a further hint that our family was not related to Jost whose descendants were quite affluent for the most part. In short, the only thing my ancestors had in common with the family of Jost Hite was a surname. Had it not been for the Revolutionary War service of my ancestor Christopher Hite (who participated in the siege of Yorktown) I would have every reason to believe that my father was the first of my direct male-line ancestors to ever set foot in the state of Virginia. Coincidentally, I was born there – my father was in the United States Army and stationed at Fort Belvoir at the time of my birth – but like so many

Americans born in the post World War II era, my birthplace says nothing about my family origins.

Nothing in Common But the Surname

Even for the Hite families not related to Jost in the Shenandoah Valley, discerning researchers could have found reasons to question a relationship to Jost before DNA testing proved there was no connection. One family, known as the "Page County Hites", traces its lineage to four men born in the 1740s, 1750s, and 1760s (Daniel, Abraham, Andrew, and John) who came from Pennsylvania to present-day Page County, Virginia as young men. These men were in the same age range as most of Jost Hite's grandsons and many researchers assumed they were nephews or grandnephews of Jost. A county history published early in the 20th century by Shenandoah Valley historian John Wayland specifically stated that they were descendants of a brother of Jost. DNA tests proved that while the four were related to each other (strengthening the case that they were brothers as widely believed), they were not related to Jost. Prior to the DNA results though, there were reasons to doubt there was a connection. Even though the area these men lived in was in the Shenandoah Valley, the area they settled in is nearly an hour's trip by automobile from the area of settlement of Jost's family. Documentation of the families reveals no evidence of interaction. Also, at least two of the so-called "Page County Hites" signed their surname in German as late as the early 19th century. Jost Hite also signed his name in German, but his sons and later generations were all literate in English well before the Revolutionary War. Like my family, the Page County Hites had virtually nothing in common with Jost Hite and his family other than a surname.

It Even Happens With Common Names

The surnames Boone, Lincoln, and Hite are not all that common so it's not entirely surprising that people with those surnames in their lineages would assume kinship with the famous people who bore the same name. Such traditions pervade families with common surnames also, however. Another surname in my lineage is Carter – the maiden name of a great-great-grandmother, Mary Ann (Carter) Grogan (1837-1907) who lived in Rockingham County, North Carolina. At this point, Mary Ann's Carter lineage is traceable only to her paternal grandfather, George Washington Carter (ca. 1780-1854) who married Sarah Gibson and lived his entire adult life in Rockingham County. At the time of the 1850 census, George's real property was valued at 500 dollars and he owned three slaves. He could not have been described as poor, but no one would have considered him wealthy either. Despite his modest means, however, many of his descendants still cling to the idea that he descended from the prominent Carter family of colonial Virginia whose best known member, Robert "King" Carter, died in 1732 holding title to more than 300,000 acres and 700 slaves. Among "King" Carter's descendants is the Confederate general Robert E. Lee and many of my relatives proudly proclaimed this kinship to me as I was growing up in an only partially reconstructed area of the South.

In 1931, descendants of George Washington Carter began holding annual reunions at Shiloh Baptist Church in Rockingham County, the church his family had attended. For the occasion, a descendant (or group of descendants) prepared a chart showing him as a great-grandson of "King" Carter by the latter's son, Charles Carter (1707-1764) of *Cleve* (a plantation) and Charles's son, another Charles Carter (1733-1796) who owned a plantation called *Ludlow*. As it happens, the younger Charles *did* have a son named George Washington Carter who was born in 1777 (about three years before the birth of my ancestor) but he died in Spotsylvania County, Virginia in 1809. His grave can be found in the Willis Cemetery in Fredericksburg, Virginia and his tombstone identifies him as the son of Charles Carter of *Ludlow*, who is buried in the same cemetery. Apparently my overeager relatives of the 1930s simply latched on to this man's name and jumped to the conclusion that this was our George Washington Carter. They obviously gave no thought to the question of why a young man from such a prominent family would leave an established plantation in eastern Virginia to carve out a living in a comparative wilderness like Rockingham County.

Disowned? Not Likely

Often, claims of kinships to such prominent families may be accompanied by a story of an ancestor being disowned for marrying someone of a lower class or someone that the prominent family might not approve of for one reason or another. In the case of George Washington Carter, there might have been a reason to suspect that. His wife Sarah Gibson (ca. 1785-1870), though apparently not from a family poorer than his, was the product of an illicit union between Elizabeth Gibson, a single young woman of Rockingham County, and a married man named Winkfield Shropshire. Records of the Court of Common Pleas of Rockingham County reveal that Shropshire was ordered to pay Elizabeth's father, Joseph Gibson "for his trouble in raising a bastard child begot on the body of Elizabeth Gibson by the said Shropshire." It is perhaps no coincidence that Shropshire moved to Georgia just a few years after Sarah's birth. Certainly George Washington Carter's parents, whoever they were, might not have been entirely thrilled with their son's choice of a bride at the time of his marriage and that may be part of the reason that no record identifying them has yet been located. This sort of event, however, does not add any credence to the idea that he was from the prominent family of "King" Carter. Families of modest means in that era were no more likely to approve of illegitimacy than prominent families were and given that existing evidence clearly disassociates George Washington Carter of Rockingham County with the son of Charles Carter of *Ludlow*, it is a waste of time to pursue that line of research any further. Such disapproval was not part of the tradition in the family of George Washington Carter anyway – possibly because later generations, if they knew of Sarah Gibson's illegitimacy, did not want to discuss it.

My grandmother and all of her siblings went to their graves believing that they were descendants of "King" Carter. They also believed themselves to be distantly related to the Confederate general Robert E. Lee, whose Carter lineage was included on the chart my relatives made in the 1930s. As late as the 1980s, when I was attending these reunions myself, the chart showing this fictitious connection was still being displayed there. I have no doubt this widespread belief has stifled serious research on the background of my ancestor George Washington Carter. I can only hope that one day I will locate his real parents among a Carter family of more modest means in North Carolina or Virginia.

Giving Up the Ghost – Don't Waste Time

The cases of Jost Hite and Robert "King" Carter demonstrate unequivocally how damaging a focus on proving connections to prominent people can be to serious genealogical research. Over the years, I have focused more attention on my Hite ancestors than my Carter lineage and I will always remember the people I met who told me "We know we're descended from Jost Hite, we just don't know how." Usually they have believed this because a parent or other older relative told them so. I have only encountered one case in which a person who made that statement later proved a connection to Jost Hite's family – the others, at least those who resolved their lineages, all turned out to be from different Hite families, many of those from the Shenandoah Valley. In the case of the Hite surname, anyone who traces back to the early nineteenth century and does not find a link to Jost's family, never will – his descendants down to that point are too well-documented. For some families, DNA testing has been the "silver bullet" that finally proved they were not descendants of Jost Hite and in my family's case, it actually took us to a specific village of origin in Germany (Grötzingen, east of Karlsruhe), nearly a two-hour train ride from Jost Hite's native village (Bonfeld, east of Bad Rappenau), though both villages are in the modern-day state of Baden-Württemburg. Another Hite family, descendants of the 1738 immigrants Conrad Heyd and his son Abraham, found their ancestral home near the town of Kusel in the Rheinland-Pfalz, an even greater distance from Jost Hite's German home. These breakthroughs only became possible because of the descendants' willingness to accept the possibility that their family did not connect to that of Jost Hite. The same is true of my Carter relatives, who have yet to identify an ancestor any earlier than George Washington Carter.

When trying to determine a relationship (or lack thereof) to a famous or prominent individual with the same surname, these are the questions to keep in mind:

1. Did my ancestors live in close proximity to the family of the famous person?
2. If not, do typical migration patterns still suggest a possible connection?
3. Was my family of a similar socioeconomic status to the family of the famous person?
4. Is there any record of interaction between my family and that of the famous person?

These questions must all be considered. Regardless of the answers one arrives at though, no genealogist should ever focus solely on the family of a famous person with the same surname when tracing his or her own ancestors. A yes answer to any of the preceding questions does not prove a relationship – it merely suggests the possibility. As an example, one of the witnesses to the will of Isaac Hite (1723-1795, a son of Jost) was Alexander Hite (1740-1813), but DNA testing has proven that Alexander was not related to Jost. The proximity of five unrelated Lincolns to Abraham Lincoln's immigrant ancestor Samuel in Hingham, Massachusetts (again proven by DNA) offers another illustration of this.

An example of a migration pattern that did not make sense combined with an inappropriate socioeconomic status involves another of my ancestors, William Royal, who died in 1794 in Sampson County, North Carolina (a county of numerous family connections for me). William, assumed to have been born in the 1720s, settled in present-day Sampson County prior to the Revolutionary War along with a contemporary named John Royal, presumed to be a brother. These two given names, common as they were, led overeager researchers to a pair of brothers by those names that were born in Henrico County, Virginia in 1724 and 1729, respectively, sons of Henry *Royall*. Henry Royall was a grandson of Joseph Royall, an immigrant who arrived from England as an indentured servant in 1622, but who rose to prominence after his term of service ended and established himself on a plantation he named *Doggams* in Charles City County, Virginia. After his death in 1658, his much-younger widow (Katherine Banks Royall) remarried to a merchant named Henry Isham and had some more children, one of whom (Mary Isham, born ca. 1659) married William Randolph and produced numerous prominent descendants, among them Thomas Jefferson and Robert E. Lee. The Royal line is an ancestral family of my maternal grandfather, Robert Wesley Williams, so both of my mother's parents descend from families that have claimed kinship to Robert E. Lee!

As with my Carter ancestors, however, this alleged lineage raised questions. Despite that, though, two articles on this Royal family appeared in the *The Heritage of Sampson County* (published in 1983) identified William Royal's son Young Royal (1755-1818) as a third cousin of Thomas Jefferson and of Henry "Light Horse Harry" Lee (the father of Robert E. Lee). The given name of Young's brother, Isham Royal (1760-1833, my ancestor) was thought to have been derived from their alleged step-great-great-grandfather, Henry Isham. However, the socioeconomic status of the Royal family of Sampson County did not fit with the prominence of their contemporaries in Henrico County. Aside from that, Sampson County was not a likely destination for people who relocated from Henrico County. People from that part of Virginia who moved on were much more likely to move southwest and if they settled in North Carolina, they were more likely to land in counties significantly further west than Sampson. Eventually, Henry Royall's son John was traced to Surry County, North Carolina where he died in 1810. This county is located nearly 200 miles west of Sampson County.

The Truth is Out There…Sometimes

So where does this leave William and John Royal of Sampson County? Luckily, other researchers did not take the connection to the 1622 immigrant Joseph Royall for granted either. Variations of the surname appeared in records of Pasquotank County, North Carolina in the early 18th century, a county in the northeastern corner of the state that is a much more likely location for early settlers of present-day Sampson County than Henrico County, Virginia was. In 1752, a lawsuit filed by John Royal of Edgecombe County, North Carolina (a former resident of Pasquotank County) proved that he had a brother named William who was still in Pasquotank County. The suit concerned the estate of their father *Cornelius* Royal, who had died about 1745 in Pasquotank County. William apparently had settled the estate to the exclusion of his brother John after Cornelius's death. Further research into this family did not absolutely prove the identity of Cornelius's parents, but it was possible to identify his wife, Elizabeth (Barnsfield) Royal and her parents, William and Ann Barnsfield, the latter of whom died in 1721 in Pasquotank County. This William Royal, son of Cornelius and Elizabeth (Barnsfield) Royal, is obviously my ancestor of that name. The other William Royal, son of Henry Royal of Henrico County, Virginia, is not my ancestor and is probably not related. That means, of course, that I and the other Royal descendants in the southeastern North Carolina counties of Sampson and Cumberland are not related to Thomas Jefferson or Robert E. Lee either.

Losing the Popularity Contest

Unlike my grandmother, my grandfather never spoke of being related to Robert E. Lee. He also never mentioned any connection to Thomas Jefferson. He probably did not know that the Royal surname was an ancestral surname of his (it was the maiden name of a great-grandmother). We did know people named Royal in the community we lived in, but I never knew we were related to them until I started my genealogical research in my late teens. There were Royals in the area, however, who knew of the claim to descent from Joseph Royall and of the alleged relationship to Jefferson and Lee very well. One of the researchers who proved the actual lineage to Cornelius Royal noted in an e-mail message that his work had not been too popular because everyone wanted to be related to the famous Royalls in Virginia. Further research on Cornelius Royal has, however, shown that he was probably a grandson of Thomas Royal (or Ryall) who died in 1709 in Isle of Wight County, Virginia, a county in the southeastern corner of the state that is an ancestral home for numerous other Sampson County, North Carolina residents – unlike Henrico County, located further northwest. This Thomas Royal, who emigrated to the colony of Virginia in 1666, had a son named John Royal who appears to have been the father of Cornelius. So the Royals of Sampson County still have roots in 17th century Virginia – just not through the immigrant Joseph Royall that they had long claimed as their ancestor.

Why Deny Truth?

Obviously, one of the worst mistakes any genealogist can make is to take a tradition of a relationship to a famous person for granted. In most cases, such assumptions only lead to frustration. The vast majority of Boones and Lincolns in the United States are not related to Daniel Boone and Abraham Lincoln and researchers who focus only on the families of those two noteworthy men will, in most cases, deny themselves the possibility of finding their actual ancestors. In my own research, I could have fallen into the same trap had I limited my search for my Hite ancestors to the descendants of Jost Hite. Many Hites I have met did make that mistake for years and have not yet experienced the success I have enjoyed in pinpointing the German village of origin of my Hite family. I have no doubt that if earlier generations of Hites in many other families had not focused so much attention on Jost, more would now be known about the ancestry of other Hite families. The same is true of my Carter ancestors. With that family, I have yet to document any ancestors earlier than George Washington Carter of Rockingham County, but I know enough about the family of "King" Carter to rule him out as a possible ancestor. Therefore, I have not wasted any effort looking further into his descendants for many years. In the case of my Royal ancestors, I was lucky enough to have distant relatives who were as skeptical of a connection to the 1622 immigrant Joseph Royall as I was about a possible connection between my Hite family and that of Jost Hite. They found our real Royal family ancestors, just as I found my actual Hite forbearers.

Eminent Scholars Trip Up

The mistake of focusing on famous individuals or families with a connected surname is not one that only amateur genealogists and other researchers make. Even accomplished scholars, whose expertise lies in areas other than genealogy, fall into the same trap at times. Noted author and journalist Gerald Posner made a mistaken assumption about the ancestry of James Earl Ray, the convicted assassin of Martin Luther King, in his 1998 book *Killing the Dream: James Earl Ray and the Assassination of Martin Luther King, Jr.* Part II of the book is primarily a biography of Ray and Posner begins it with a brief account of the assassin's background. He said of Ray "His father's side of the family had a nearly one-hundred-year unbroken history of violence and run-ins with the law. Ned Ray, hanged for being part of the notorious Plummer gang, which killed over a hundred men in a series of brutal mid-1800s robberies, was likely James's great-grandfather."[3] Posner bases this claim on a statement made by George "Speedy" Ray, the assassin's father, when talking to author George McMillan. The elder Ray, on being told the story of Ned Ray, responded that the history "sounds right, just like what my old man used to tell me about his father." Posner goes on to say that "Poor rural families like the Rays do not normally keep family trees, diaries, letters, or written records, but Ray's father (George) was the keeper of the family's oral history."[4]

Posner's statement about poor rural families and private papers is certainly accurate, but it also illustrates that, at least at the time of writing his book, he had virtually no awareness of genealogical data available in public records. He apparently never took the time to check census records and vital records, which list everyone, regardless of their economic status. If Posner had been aware of those sources and had utilized them, he would have learned that it was not possible for the aforementioned Ned Ray to have been the great-grandfather of James Earl Ray.

Ned Ray was hanged in Bannack, Montana in 1864 by a group of vigilantes, having been suspected (perhaps rightfully so) of being a part of a group of outlaws who robbed travelers of gold and killed any witnesses to their crimes. The reputed leader, Henry Plummer, was sheriff in Bannack and so their crimes went unpunished until

---

[33] Gerald Posner, *Killing the Dream: James Earl Ray and the Assassination of Martin Luther King, Jr.* (San Diego, CA: Harcourt, Brace, and Company, 1998), p. 77.
[44] Posner, p. 77.

vigilantes became involved and hanged Plummer, Ray, and some others. Posner saw this as the beginning of involvement in crime of the paternal ancestors of James Earl Ray.

A bit of genealogical research, however, could have quickly demonstrated to Posner that this lineage was impossible. James Earl Ray's grandfather, James Ray, was born in 1871 in Pike County, Illinois as evidenced by census records and his death certificate, filed after he died in Quincy, Illinois in 1947. Ned Ray, hanged in 1864, certainly could not have fathered a son who was born in 1871. A search of basic genealogy sources would have rendered that idea obsolete anyway. The 1880 census shows James Ray, age 8 (the assassin's grandfather) residing in the household of his own father, also named James Ray, who had been born in Illinois about 1840. The 1947 death certificate of the younger James Ray (age 8 in 1880) also identifies his father as James Ray. Even though information on parents that appears on death certificates is, in and of itself, oral history, it matches the census records in this case which gives it added credibility. So to sum up, the great-grandfather of Martin Luther King's assassin, James Earl Ray, was James Ray of Illinois, not Ned Ray who was hanged in Montana in 1864. While this elder James Ray, born in the early 1840s, may have run afoul of the law at some point in his life, he is highly unlikely to have been hanged. In 1910, at the age of about 70, he was living quietly in Quincy, Illinois with a daughter and son-in-law. It is surprising that his grandson George "Speedy" Ray, who was ten years old at the and also lived in Quincy, knew no more about him than he did. Perhaps the assassin's father enjoyed the media attention that his son's notoriety brought and played it for all it was worth. Ned Ray, who Speedy claimed as his grandfather, was probably not even related to him, at least not closely. Geography suggests that there was no relation at all. Clearly, even established scholars like Gerald Posner can err in assuming that oral history is correct without checking the appropriate sources first.

The Connection May be More Distant

All of the aforementioned cases involve claims of relationships with people that turned out not to be related at all. Researchers must also consider the possibility that even if they are related to the famous people with the same surname, the relationship might not be as close as some in the family would have them believe. I have encountered this often in my own research, even with surnames that are quite common. As it happens, my immediate Williams family does include someone who was quite well-known at one time – David Marshall "Carbine" Williams (1900-1975), a brother of my maternal grandfather, Robert Wesley Williams (1905-1972). I never had to research this connection – I grew up within a mile of this great-uncle's home and I knew him and his wife well. He was one of the principal designers of the M1 Carbine that was the rifle primarily used by American troops during World War II. He invented his first gun while in prison for a second-degree murder conviction, a result of a raid on a still he operated during the early 1920s. A deputy was killed during the raid. In the early 1950s, a movie about him titled simply *Carbine Williams* was filmed with Jimmy Stewart in the title role. About a decade ago, I responded to a query about him on Genforum, posted by someone whose father (a Williams) had told her Carbine Williams was his cousin. She was able to give me the names of her grandfather and great-grandfather – fortunately, she had first and middle names and neither of the first names were common ones. As it turned out, there was a connection – Carbine and I have a common ancestor with these people in the person of John Williams, who died in 1783 in present-day Sampson County, North Carolina. That relationship is obviously not one that would be close enough for anyone in this woman's family to have grown up with Carbine and known him as a cousin – they apparently had simply heard of him, knew he was from the same general vicinity as their family, and wondered if they were related.

My response on Genforum quickly generated a few more inquiries. I received one from a man whose grandmother's maiden name was Sarah Williams. She had been a contemporary of Carbine. This man apparently had not remembered his Williams grandmother very well (if at all) but his other grandmother had told him that Sarah Williams was a sister of Carbine. He was smart enough not to take that for granted and he e-mailed me to ask. I had personally known all of Carbine's sisters so I was able to tell him immediately that his other grandmother's assertion had been false – which did not surprise him. My aforementioned cousin, John C. Rosser, Jr., had published a book on our Williams family in 1990 titled *Coharie to Cape Fear: The Descendants of John Williams and Katherine Galbreth of Sampson and Cumberland Counties in North Carolina (1740-1990)*. I did find his grandmother in this book and she was a fifth cousin to Carbine – more closely related to the person who posted the query I responded to than to Carbine or me. In both cases, the researchers were pleased with what I gave them. Even though I had dispelled their family's tradition of a close relationship to Carbine Williams, I had been able to provide them both with several generations of their Williams lineage that they did not previously have. Far less importantly to both of them, I was also able to tell them that they were, after all, related to Carbine Williams – just not as closely as they had been led to believe.

Not an Uncle – But Related

A similar situation arose concerning a tradition in my immediate family involving William Rufus DeVane King (1786-1853) who was elected Vice-President of the United States in 1852, along with Franklin Pierce as President. The mother of my maternal grandfather (Robert Wesley Williams) and Carbine Williams was Laura Susan (Kornegay) Williams (1874-1947) and her mother was Sallie Ann Ophelia (King) Kornegay (1851-1901). These Kornegays and Kings all lived in Sampson County, North Carolina and William R.D. King, though a resident of Alabama by the time of his election to the Vice-Presidency, was a native of that county. One of my earliest childhood memories relating to genealogy was being told that he was a distant uncle. This piece of oral history found its way into print in a biography of Carbine Williams, published by Ross E. Beard, Jr. in 1977 – *Carbine: The Story of David Marshall Williams*. This book includes a photo of William Rufus King and identifies him as a great-great-uncle of Carbine Williams.

Research of my King ancestry told a different story, however. Sallie Ann Ophelia King's father was David Cogdell King (ca. 1822-1872) and her paternal grandfather, who was a contemporary of the Vice-President, was John King (1789-1844). Based on family tradition, we would have expected John King to have been a brother of William Rufus. But he was not. The Vice-President's father was named William King and John's father, as shown by a family Bible and other sources, was Stephen King (1756-1812) of Sampson County. So were they first cousins? Again, the answer was no. The elder William's father was named Michael King and Stephen's father was Henry King (ca. 1722-1762). Finally, going back one more generation produced an answer. Michael and Henry King were brothers, sons of an older Michael King (ca. 1698-1742) of Bertie County, North Carolina, a county located in the northeastern corner of the state more than 100 miles north of present-day Sampson County. The younger Michael and his brother Henry married sisters named Snell (daughters of Roger Snell) and moved with their father-in-law to the area that later became Sampson County. The end result of this was that Vice-President King was a second cousin of my ancestor John King. He was related – but not as a distant uncle as I and my grandfather's generation had been led to believe.

Further research into other branches of the family did lead to some possible sources of the confusion. My direct ancestor David Cogdell King (John's son) *did* have a brother named William Rufus King who was born in 1812 – a generation after the Vice-President. The two men could have easily become confused in discussions of family relationships after their lifetimes. Another possible source of the misinformation as that the Vice-President *did* have a sister, Tabitha, who married a man named Kornegay – Basil Kornegay to be specific. Kornegay was, as I already mentioned, the maiden name of my great-grandmother. Vice-President King, who never married or had children, named his sister Tabitha Kornegay in his will and I have a very clear memory of my uncle showing me a transcription of the will when I was first becoming interested in genealogy. He gave me the impression that Tabitha Kornegay and her husband Basil might be our direct ancestors. Research into our Kornegay lineage, however, led me not to Basil Kornegay, but to his brother Jacob Kornegay who died in 1816. Jacob's wife was a Wiggins, not a King, so there was no additional King connection for us through that line. William Rufus DeVane King was not a distant uncle to me – instead, he was a second cousin six times removed.

Situations such as this also illustrate the risks inherent in focusing on famous people bearing a surname one is researching. These scenarios are slightly different than the previous ones in that a relationship to a noteworthy individual *was* found. The relationships were not as close as earlier generations of the family had believed though. Had I accepted without question that William Rufus DeVane King was a distant uncle, I would have fallen into a trap of looking only at the descendants of his brothers for my King ancestors – and I might still be looking to this day, even if I had found the father of Sallie Ann Ophelia King from census records, which was easy to do. By the same token, I could have assumed that I was a direct descendant of Basil and Tabitha (King) Kornegay rather than Basil's brother Jacob and his wife Elizabeth Wiggins. Such an assumption would have kept me from learning of my connection to Elizabeth's father, a Revolutionary War soldier named Willis Wiggins. Genealogists who focus only on well-known names run the risk of never finding their actual ancestors.

37

Don't Miss Out

There is always the chance that genealogists *will* find a connection to someone famous with the same surname they are researching (or, for that matter, a different surname). That possibility should never be ruled out, but it should also never be taken for granted. Far too many genealogists make the critical mistake of focusing only on famous people with the surnames they are searching and focusing so narrowly most often denies them the opportunity to find their actual ancestors. In many cases, the relatively obscure people that we actually are descendants of are just as interesting, if not more so, than the famous ones. I am not a descendant of Jost Hite. I am, however, a descendant of Christopher Hite (ca. 1759-1827) who, while never wealthy, served more than six years in the Continental Army during the Revolutionary War and participated in some of its most crucial battles. My German Heidt (or Heyd) ancestors did not come from Jost Hite's native village of Bonfeld (near Bad Wimpfen) but they did come from the village of Grötzingen (east of the city of Karlsruhe) where the Heidt/Heyd surname can be found in records as early as 1482. On my most recent visit to Grötzingen, my distant cousin Siegfried Heidt led me to the very hills in the village where these early bearers of our surname owned partial interests in vineyards more than five centuries ago. Had I confined my research to Jost Hite's children and grandchildren, I never would have been to Grötzingen or met Siegfried and his family who have now hosted me in their home in my ancestral village on three separate occasions. The potential rewards of finding one's actual ancestors are too many to deny oneself the possibility by focusing only on the rich and famous.

Chapter 5 - Relationships to Royalty, Nobility, or Wealth

At first glance, it may appear that this chapter examines the same issue as the previous one. That is not the case. The previous chapter concentrates on instances of focusing one's research on a famous person with the same surname that the genealogist is pursuing. The traditions this chapter addresses involve stories of descent from royalty, nobility, or persons of wealth and/or prominence. Often, in these cases, the surnames of the alleged noteworthy ancestors are not even known – the allegation of their status is all that a family's budding genealogist has heard.

We're All Royalty Somehow

It is worthwhile to note at this point that nearly everyone of primarily European background *is* a descendant of European royalty and/or nobility somehow. Statistically, geneticists feel safe in assuming that everyone of that background alive today is somehow a descendant of Charlemagne (King of the Franks from 768 until his death in 814 and Emperor of the Romans – a title that was forerunner of *Holy Roman Emperor* - from 800 until 814). Tracing one's lineages far back enough to identify that link is often a huge challenge and if that is what one is specifically looking for, choosing the correct lineage to trace in order to find it is often a shot in the dark. Most genealogists who find that link happen onto it accidentally.

That is how I found my own link to the European royal families (the only one I have located so far and I found it only after twenty-four years of research). I was trying to identify the ancestors of Mark Cook, who died between 1780 and 1782 in Sussex County, Delaware, the earliest known direct male-line ancestor of my great-grandmother Emma Catherine (Cook) Hite. I knew he had died young, leaving a widow and three minor children, among them Emma's great-grandfather, Thomas Patterson Cook (ca. 1780-1840). I was not having any luck finding Mark's Cook ancestors, but I did stumble across a reference to some deeds in Dorchester County, Maryland (where he had previously lived) that identified him and his wife Sabarina as heirs of Thomas *Pattison*, who had died about 1774 in Dorchester County. It was obvious that Thomas Patterson Cook had been named for his maternal grandfather, with his middle name having been altered slightly from the earlier spelling of his mother's maiden name. Having found only frustration in my search for Cooks, I turned my attention to the Pattisons and quickly found that the Thomas Pattison who had died in 1774 had been the son of an earlier Thomas Pattison and his wife Sarah Codd. Sarah, in turn, was a daughter of an immigrant named St. Leger Codd (his given name was the maiden name of his mother Mary St. Leger), born in England in 1635 who arrived in Lancaster County, Virginia by 1670. Codd later moved to Northumberland County, Virginia and then to Cecil County, Maryland where he died in 1706. His English ancestry on his mother's side is well-documented and includes no fewer than seven separate lineages back to King Edward III, who reigned from 1327 to 1377. I had found royal ancestry completely by accident.

But Finding Proof is Usually Just Pure Luck

It is ironic in many ways that Emma Catherine (Cook) Hite would turn out to be the great-grandparent whose background led me to this link. When I began working on my genealogy, I knew less about her than any of my other seven great-grandparents and she was the last one whose parents I had identified. I had long been under the impression that her ancestors had been among the most impoverished of any in my lineage but I now know that is not the case. If anything, her background is more prominent than that of her husband, William Henry Albert Hite. Her childhood circumstances were troubled – but this was primarily because of the early deaths of both of her parents. Her father, Elijah N. Cook, died two weeks before her birth and her mother, Sarah Ann (Worley) Cook died a month after she was born. Even though her ancestors had turned out not to be as obscure as I expected, I had no reason to think she was of royal descent until I literally stumbled onto it.

There was actually no tradition I had ever heard of royal or noble ancestry anywhere in my lineage. I have encountered other researchers, however, who have known of such traditions in their families and searched very hard for them – usually without success. In some cases, I have encountered researchers who published such traditions as factual without really bothering to delve into them. Very often, the traditions involve a legend of someone who was disowned for marrying beneath his or her station in life. I particularly remember a story that a student I once worked with told me of a great-great-great-grandmother who had been a duchess in Germany and had been disinherited when she married her guard, leading both of them to move to the Canadian province of Ontario - the town of Guelph to be specific. He knew the name of the great-great-great grandfather involved (the alleged guard) as Lorry Warner, but he did not know the name of his wife, the supposed duchess. Fortunately, he delved into primary sources in an effort to determine truth of the matter. The sources that he and I checked told a far different story. He had the exact date of birth for Lorry Warner's son George (12 January 1878) and so he ordered the microfilm for birth records for Guelph.

George Warner's birth record gave his father's name as *Elisha* Warner and his mother's maiden name as Isabella Emory. Neither parent's name hinted at German origins. The surname *Warner* could always be an anglicized version of *Werner*, but *Elisha* seems unlikely to have been an anglicized version of any German given name for men. Further research was obviously necessary. The 1881 census of Guelph, Ontario showed the three-year old George Warner with his parents Elisha and Isabella, born ca. 1856 and 1857, respectively, both in Ontario. Furthermore, the census indicated that both parents were of English descent, as one would expect with those surnames and given names. The next step was to find the marriage record of Elisha and Isabella. Elisha *Loree* Warner (perhaps he was later known by his middle name), age 20, born in the township of Eramosa (in Wellington County, Ontario), son of Andrew and Lydia Marie Warner, married 5 July 1876 in Georgetown, Ontario to Isabella Emory, age 20, born in Waterdown, Ontario, daughter of John and Annie Emory. To sum up, the alleged German duchess and the guard she fell in love with and married, were both born in the

Canadian province of Ontario and were both of English descent. In the case of Elisha Loree Warner, his parents Andrew and Lydia Marie were both also born in Ontario, in 1821 and 1825, respectively (no further information has yet been located on Isabella Emory's family). The resolution of this question gave no clue as to where the tradition of the German duchess and her guard might have come from.

And it's Probably Not a Recent Descent

One of the things that made this story suspicious from the start was how recent the alleged connection to nobility had been. Most modern European-Americans who can document their descent from royalty and nobility find it much further in the past than that. For anyone who like myself who is almost entirely (and perhaps entirely) of pre-Revolutionary War American ancestry, any alleged connection to a European monarch more recent than Edward III (or nobility from an era later than his) must be eyed with extreme suspicion. For some who descend from 19th and early 20th century immigrants, connections to more recent monarchs and nobles may be somewhat more likely (the television series *Who Do You Think You Are* revealed that the actress Brooke Shields, for example, is a descendant of the French king Henri IV who reigned from 1589 until 1610) but a claim to descent from a 19th century monarch or noble by any American must be carefully examined.

I have encountered other researchers through the years with similar stories of descent from later royalty. One researcher I came to know while living in Columbus, Ohio, described a family tradition (which she had serious doubts about) that her Ames ancestors were descendants of an illegitimate son of Britain's King James I, who reigned from 1603 to 1625. The name "Ames" she had been told, had resulted from dropping the letter "J" from *James*. She regarded the story as a bit of a stretch, but was not discounting it. I remembered something, however, from a class I took in graduate school on Tudor and Stuart England that she did not know. King James I, while he undoubtedly had extramarital affairs just as most monarchs of his era did, is far less likely to have produced illegitimate children than the others are. The reason is simple – he was gay. His illicit affairs – at least the vast majority of them if not all - were with men, not women. It is also true that monarchs of James's era usually acknowledged illegitimate children so if James did have an illegitimate son, there would have been no reason for him to subtly conceal the boy's identity by giving him the surname "Ames". It was assumed that kings would have extramarital affairs and produce children by mistresses. In the case of King James I, it would have actually been advantageous to acknowledge such children. Rumors of his proclivity for men *were* harmful – just as they had been for his ancestor Edward II, who had reigned from 1307 to 1327. Fathering a few illegitimate children might not have completely squelched rumors of James's sexual orientation, but they would have cast doubts on them.

Even if James I had not been gay, the story of him having an illegitimate child with descendants who came to America during the colonial era would have been questionable. Illegitimate children of monarchs did not stand in line for the throne, but they were usually provided for enough to ensure them a standard of living that gave them no reason to leave their European homes. Many were endowed with noble titles, even if their mothers had no known nobility in their ancestry. Several generations were likely to pass before descendants found themselves in reduced circumstances. Only then would any of them have been likely to make the trek to the American colonies (or later, to the United States). Very few colonial era immigrants to the colonies are documented to any English king more recent than Edward III. Therefore, any tradition of such a descent must be eyed skeptically – and traditions involving earlier monarchs demand documentation.

The same situation that applies to alleged lineages to European royalty also applies to nobility. Certainly, there are numerous descendants of signers of England's Magna Carta in the United States and that was true even in the colonial era. The Magna Carta was signed in the year 1215, nearly four hundred years before the first English settlements in the colonies, so it is not surprising that most of them would have descendants who were no longer living in the best of circumstances by that time. Claims to descent from recent nobility in the United States, however, raise questions, and jumping to rash conclusions based on sketchy stories is not at all unusual. Once, while researching in Indiana, I encountered a couple with the surname *Essex*. They had a typed genealogy of their family that stated as fact an allegation that their Essex family descended from one of two disowned sons of an English Earl of Essex from the 17th century. The typescript did include a transcription of a will of an Earl of Essex from that era that noted he was disinheriting two of his sons. The will did not, however, identify the sons by name. How they made the leap of faith that their ancestor was one of these sons and that he had taken Essex as his surname was not explained to me. It is not, however, a conjecture I would accept as proven.

The Least Likely Explanation – Someone Was Disowned

The idea that an ancestor was "disowned" is a common oral tradition. Often, the ancestor in question is not even identified by name. The stories of men of average means marrying women who were the daughters of wealthy landowners that did not approve of the marriage are many – though it is rare that these women are identified by surname. Very often, such stories arise from female ancestors whose maiden names prove elusive to their descendants. Indeed, depending on where one's ancestors lived, determining maiden names of female forbearers is often one of the greatest challenges genealogists face. But to assume that a difficult-to-identify ancestor was disowned is not a leap of faith I would make. Such difficulties more often indicate that ancestors came from families of lesser means than from wealth - their fathers' estates may not have been significant enough to warrant detailed documentation of their distribution. Another possibility that must be considered in the case of elusive female ancestors is that their fathers died before they married and thus, they are identified only by their maiden names in the will or estate file. When a researcher does not know the maiden name of a female ancestor, this does not help with the search.

There is a story involving a connection to prominence involving some of my own ancestors in North Carolina. One of my great-grandmothers, Laura Susan (Kornegay)

Williams (1874-1947) was a descendant of George Kornegay (original surname possibly Gnäge), a German who arrived in New Bern, North Carolina in 1710 along with several hundred other German settlers who had left the Reich for Great Britain the previous year. The tradition involves the wife of this George's son, also named George Kornegay. To this point, I have not found any documentation to positively identify the younger George Kornegay's wife even though he rose to prominence and produced numerous descendants that resided in the southeastern North Carolina counties of Duplin, Wayne, and Sampson (the birthplace of my great-grandmother Laura). According to the legend, the second George's wife was Margaret (Downing) Lullum, the widow of a sea captain named Lullum and a descendant of the Downing family of 10 Downing Street in London (the residence of British prime ministers). Some versions of the story even go as far as to identify her as a daughter of George Downing (1623-1684), a son of Emanuel and Lucy (Winthrop) Downing and a nephew of Massachusetts founder John Winthrop. Chronology proves that connection is impossible. The second George Kornegay was born no earlier than the 1720s (more likely in the 1730s) and would hardly have been married to a woman whose father had died in 1684. If the younger George Kornegay's wife *was* a descendant of this family (one published genealogy gave her father's name as Robert Downing rather than George) no proof has yet surfaced. It *is* possible that her maiden name was Downing and that she was the widow of a Lullum or had some other tie to the family – both of those surnames appears as middle names for some of her descendants – but that all important documentation remains elusive.

The connections to royalty, nobility, and wealth are there for most Americans. For most of us, however, the connections are not very recent and finding them is more often a matter of luck than anything else – as it was for me in discovering a connection to St. Leger Codd, my immigrant ancestor of royal descent. Like the assumed connections to famous people of the same name, genealogists who focus only on finding lineages to ancestors with such bloodlines will usually find only frustration, even if family oral traditions proclaim their truth. Like anything else in genealogy, researchers should just continue down whatever paths they find – and if a path does lead one to a royal, noble, or wealthy ancestor, it will be found.

Chapter 6 - Birthplaces of Ancestors

Establishing an ancestor's birthplace is, for obvious reasons, an important step in genealogical research. For many modern-day Americans, their birthplaces mean little in terms of their family's origins because people are so mobile now. I am an example of this myself, having been born in Fort Belvoir, Virginia, the military base where my father was stationed at the time of my birth. I also happen to have very deep roots in Virginia – some even in Fairfax County where Fort Belvoir is located - but that has nothing to do with the fact that I was born there. Prior to the twentieth century, however, the birthplaces of most Americans revealed much about their origins. For that reason, birthplaces of ancestors that one is told about by older relatives when beginning genealogical research demand verification. Even when the birthplaces cited turn out to be incorrect for the specific person noted, however, researchers must consider the possibility that they have some meaning in terms of the family's origins.

My father and I began our genealogical research during the summer before my senior year in high school. We were traveling from North Carolina, where we had lived since I was less than two years old, to his childhood home in Topeka, Kansas. I had met my grandmother, Jessie Bagley Hite, twice before, when she had visited us in North Carolina but this was my first trip to Kansas and I was quite excited at the prospect. Along the way, we intended to visit areas that we thought might be homes of our Hite ancestors prior to our arrival in Kansas.

Our first stop was Virginia's Shenandoah Valley, the home of Jost Hite and his family. We had no tradition of a family connection there but like all beginning Hite researchers, we had learned of the prominent Hite family there and had jumped to a conclusion that they were probably our ancestors. From there, we went on to Bloomington, Indiana which, according to some notes my dad had found, might have been the birthplace of my great-grandfather, William Henry Albert Hite, who was born in 1865.

The source for these notes had been a conversation my dad had engaged in with my grandmother about fifteen years earlier – the same one that produced his listing of her great-grandparents. My grandfather and all of his siblings had died before my dad reached adulthood, so he had no actual older Hite relatives to question about their background. Knowing what I know now, I realize that we never should have considered my grandmother a good source of information on the Hites – she and my grandfather had not grown up in the same region of the country, she had never known his mother, and his father had only lived for the first seven years of their marriage. Beginners that we were at the time, though, we drove a few hours out of our way to stop in Bloomington.

As fate had it, we did, indeed, find that a significant number of Hites had lived in Monroe County, the county Bloomington served as the seat of, in the 19th century. The given name William – my great-grandfather's name – was used in the family. We were not entirely sure our William had been born there himself, but we had the impression that even if he had not been, his parents had probably lived there before his birth. I will never forget the brief thrill I felt when Dad found a transcribed listing of the 1870 census that showed a one-year old named William Hite in the household of his 27-year old father (also named William Hite). Dad had to hastily remind me that his grandfather William had been born in 1865, not 1869 and although I wondered if that date might be wrong, he assured me that it was not. We stopped by some cemeteries in the area and also happened upon the postmaster in the small town of Stinesville, west of Bloomington, who was also a local historian. We copied a few pages of notes he had on the Hites of the area. We also found something that, in our eyes, strengthened the case for a connection between our Hites and the prominent Hites of the Shenandoah Valley. In one of the cemeteries we visited, we found tombstones for people with the surname Bowman. In our brief stop in the Shenandoah Valley, we had learned that one of Jost Hite's daughters had married a Bowman.

It Was Just a Grocery Store

Armed with this knowledge, we arrived at my grandmother's apartment in Topeka. I was eager to share what we had found, but Dad insisted we not spring it on Grandma immediately. He knew she would be eager just to talk about how everyone else in the family was doing first. When I woke up the next morning though, I found that he was only slightly more patient than I had been. He had spread out the notes we had taken in the hope that some of the names and places would spark Grandma's memory.

To our disappointment though, none of the names from the Monroe County Hite family meant anything to her. She was non-committal on the question of whether her father-in-law or any of his family had been from that area. Her explanation for her earlier suggestion of Bloomington turned out to be the fact that on a bus trip east to visit her own relatives many years earlier, she had spotted a store called *Hite Grocery* somewhere around Bloomington. Dad and I quickly realized we had probably been on a wild goose chase.

We had an entire week in Kansas though and Grandma did know where my grandfather's parents were buried. The three of us took the hour trip to the cemetery and while there, we spotted the grave of a Catherine Ann Hite (1832-1917). Grandma did not know who she was, but we knew she was in the correct age range to be William's mother. She was buried next to a couple named Fred and Emma Makadanz. Grandma knew that Emma had been a sister of William Hite, so we were sure we had found his mother. Driving around the area, we spotted mailboxes with the surname of Makadanz on them and in the yard of one of the houses, an elderly man was seated on a chair tinkering with a lawn mower. We stopped and Grandma got out of the car and approached the man. I heard her ask if he was Emma Makadanz's son. He nodded his head and as Grandma stuck out her hand and introduced herself, Dad and I hopped out of the car and dashed over.

This gentleman, whose name was Fred Makadanz, was not quite as helpful initially as we hoped. He did confirm that Catherine Hite was his grandmother, but he had never known his grandfather Hite and could not tell us his name. He did know, however, that his mother had grown up in El Dorado, Kansas, a place I had never heard of and Dad had never visited. That was the clue we needed. The very next day we went to the Kansas State Historical Society, checked the 1880 census of Butler County, Kansas (the county El Dorado is located in) and found William Hite and his parents. Their names were Daniel and Catherine and they were both born in Ohio, as were their first five children. The next two (which included our William) were born in Illinois and the youngest – Emma – had been born in Kansas. So our Hites, in their westward travels, had bypassed Indiana entirely. This census record also gave us our first hint that we might not be connected to the Hites of the Shenandoah Valley. Daniel Hite, born about 1831 according to the census, had given the birthplace of both of his parents as Pennsylvania – not Virginia as we had come to expect. I have since learned not to take birthplaces of subjects' parents given in census records as gospel – but in this particular case, the entry eventually proved to be correct.

People in the Know

Years later, I learned that the Hites of Monroe County, Indiana were of English, rather than German origin and that not only were they not our ancestors, they were not from the Shenandoah Valley Hite clan either. My dad and I were very lucky in this case – we quickly learned that the story of my great-grandfather's birth in Bloomington, Indiana was false. I must, in all honesty, credit our success to other factors besides luck. Had we not kept on open mind on that subject, we might have pursued false leads in that area for years. Knowing what I know now, of course, I never would have regarded my grandmother as a good source of information on my grandfather's family history in the first place. I already mentioned that she did not grow up in the same community that he did. Her father-in-law had only been alive for the first few years of her marriage and while she and my grandfather did live in close proximity to him – he even lived in a little hut he built behind their house for the last few years of his life – she did not have a good relationship with him and did not go out of her way to converse with him. My grandfather's cousin, Fred Makadanz, was a more obvious source of information and even though he had not been about to tell us the name of his maternal grandfather – Daniel Hite – he did point us to the county in Kansas where his mother (my great-grandfather's sister) had grown up. My grandmother had known the married name of my grandfather's aunt and that had led us to Fred Makadanz. Often, the most valuable part of oral history one can get is that which leads to other sources of information.

In the case of my Hite ancestors, my dad and I learned that Bloomington, Indiana had nothing whatsoever to do with our background. Another case of a mistakenly identified birthplace occurred in my research of the family of Melba Grogan Williams, my maternal grandmother. In this case, she provided misinformation about the birthplace of her own mother and one of her sisters corroborated it. Both of them told me that their mother, Mary Ella (Stewart) Grogan (1876-1939) had been born in Wythe County, Virginia although she lived her adult life in Rockingham County, North Carolina. Mary's death certificate also indicated that she had been born in Virginia, but did not identify a specific county. The informant for the death certificate was yet another of my grandmother's sisters who had died by the time I undertook this research.

47

This information led me to check for Stewarts in Wythe County, Virginia. My grandmother did give me the name of her maternal grandfather – James K. Polk Stewart – even though she had no memory of him. I looked at the International Genealogical Index and found a James Stuart, born in 1851, a son of a George Stuart. The spelling did not match but I knew enough by that time that the spelling of surnames was not always consistent. I knew that Mary was the oldest of several daughters in her family and that she had had a brother named George, so this James Stuart, aged 25 when she was born with a father named George, seemed a prime candidate. I had noted that the administration of President James K. Polk, my great-great-grandfather Stewart's namesake, had ended in 1849 so that cast a bit of doubt in my mind about a boy born in 1851 having that name. When I mentioned it to my grandmother, she thought I might have located the correct James – but she did not know enough to confirm or deny it. I did not take it for granted that I had located the correct James, but I certainly kept the possibility in mind.

Eventually, though, I looked up Mary and her husband, Thomas Robert Grogan on census records in Reidsville, North Carolina. The 1910 census gave her birthplace as North Carolina, not Virginia. This record also gave the birthplace of both of her parents as North Carolina. I thought little of it at first – birthplaces on census records can be wrong – one never knows who in the household supplied the information. Later, though, I literally stumbled across Mary's parents, James and Mary Etta (Bolling) Stewart in Rockingham County in the 1870 census. James's place of birth was given as North Carolina and Mary Etta's was given as Virginia. Newlyweds in 1870, they lived next door to Mary Etta's parents, William and Elizabeth (Martin) Bolling.

This discovery raised all kinds of questions, some of which I already discussed in a previous chapter. Most pertinent to the question of birthplaces, though, was that if Mary Ella Stewart was born in 1876 in Wythe County, Virginia, it seemed odd that her parents would have been in the Rockingham County – the county Mary spent her adult life in – six years before she was born. The next logical step was to locate her and her parents in 1880. That proved a challenge but eventually I found them – in Stokes County, North Carolina, the county just west of Rockingham. The problem was that Mary's father was listed by his middle name – Polk – on the 1880 census. By that time, James K. Polk and Mary Etta (Bolling) Stewart were the parents of five children – including my great-grandmother Mary – all born in North Carolina. Wythe County, Virginia is at least an hour's drive from this area of North Carolina today. There was no reason for me to believe that any of James and Mary Etta's children were born anywhere other than the North Carolina counties of Rockingham and Stokes.

Right Place – Wrong Generation

So where did the tradition of Mary Ella Stewart's birth in Wythe County, Virginia originate? The most likely answer is *her* mother's origin. In 1850, Mary Etta Bolling's parents, William and Elizabeth (Martin) Bolling appeared on the census of Pulaski County, Virginia. Wythe County borders Pulaski County. By 1860, these Bollings had moved to Surry County, North Carolina but several more children – including Mary Etta – had been born to them in the intervening decade and all but the youngest had been born in Virginia. So Mary Ella Stewart's mother was probably born in Pulaski County, Virginia or perhaps in neighboring Wythe County if the family made another move before the one to North Carolina. Somehow, my grandmother and her sisters apparently confused their mother's birthplace with that of their grandmother.

Looking back on this, I can understand why they were unclear on the question of their mother's birthplace. None of them had known their maternal grandmother, Mary Etta, and their grandfather had died when they were all small children – my grandmother had no memory of him at all and one of her older sisters had only a vague memory of him holding her on his lap. They were all adults when their mother died but it may be that they simply heard talk of family origins in or near Wythe County, Virginia and assumed it was where their mother had been born without asking her directly. In this case, unlike the false association of my Hite ancestors with Bloomington, Indiana, the Wythe County connection may have meant something.

The preceding examples of inaccurate birthplaces for two of my great-grandparents came from what is most commonly referred to as oral history – that which older relatives tell us. I have encountered inaccurate birthplaces in "written oral history" as well though. In my research for the book I wrote on the descendants of my ancestors Christopher and Margaret Hite of Bedford County, Pennsylvania, I ran across several such examples in county history accounts of their descendants. The majority of their male line descendants – my branch included – spell the surname as *Hite*. The descendants of one of their sons – George (born ca. 1795) – spell the surname as *Hight*, however and this appears to have been a conscious choice on George's part. He signed his name as *George Hight* on the document in this father's estate file that indicated he had received his share of the proceeds of the sale of the personal property. He had six brothers – all but one literate like him – and they all spelled their surname as *Hite*. George left Pennsylvania for Ohio a few years after his parents' deaths, settling first in Wayne County and then later in Lucas County. Eventually, he moved on to Pulaski County, Indiana, leaving his eldest son John (who had already married and started a family) in Lucas County. John Hight was born in 1820, unquestionably in Bedford County, where his father was listed on a tax list and as a household head on the 1820 census.

Beware of Published County Histories

A published history of Lucas County included an article about John Hight, who served in the Union Army in the Civil War along with his oldest son Albert. The book named him, both of his wives, and all of his children accurately – not surprisingly, the book was written during the lifetime of most of his children. It also named some of his siblings and it was correct about their names. The story did include a significant error though – it identified John's birthplace as Lancaster County, Pennsylvania – a county more than 100 miles east of Bedford County.

To this day, I have no idea where the idea of John Hight's birth in Lancaster County came from. There is no evidence that any of the earlier generations of the Hite/Hight family had any ties to Lancaster County. It is possible that one or both of his wives had ties there. As I read this, I could not help but wonder how many of his descendants (and perhaps those of some of his siblings) had been led astray in their research by this false birthplace. The fact that John's father spelled his surname differently than any of his brothers did complicates this family's research enough. This inaccurate information in the published Lucas County history can only have made matters worse. Fortunately, I have established contacts with a few descendants of this family and given them the correct information about their background. I can only hope this information will spread.

Another branch of the family recorded misinformation in another area of the country. David Hite (1799-1868), another son of Christopher and Margaret, relocated to Benton County, Iowa in 1850. The family became quite prominent there – in fact, this branch was the most prosperous of all of the branches of Christopher and Margaret Hite's descendants. Biographies of several of David's sons appeared in a history of Benton County that was published in the twentieth century. The information on them, their wives, and their children was all accurate and they were all correctly identified as children of David and Margaret (Stephens) Hite. One of the biographical sketches, that of Jacob Hite, accurately gives David's father's name as Christopher Hite and it also correctly notes that Christopher served seven years in the Continental Army in the Revolutionary War. Some of the other biographies in the book, however, include an inaccuracy. When mentioning David Hite, they often refer to his father (without naming him) as a native of Germany. Christopher was, indeed, of German background, but it is clear that he was born in the American colonies about 1759 – most likely in Pennsylvania. At the time of his birth, his father John Hite (Johannes Heytt or Heyd) had only been in the colonies for a few years, having arrived in Philadelphia in 1751.

This is a case in which knowledge of history helps in genealogy. Historians familiar with colonial Pennsylvania know that while there was significant German emigration into the colony from the 1680s until 1754, this immigration virtually stopped at that point and did not resume until 1764. This stoppage was because of the French and Indian War. Christopher's younger brother, Conrad Hite, applied for a Revolutionary War pension in 1832. In his own deposition, he clearly stated that he was born in the town of Bedford in Bedford County 1 January 1763. That is a clear indication that his parents were already in the colonies by 1763 and knowing that, one can only conclude that they were not still in Germany in 1759. Even if a researcher did not know the actual date of Johannes Heytt's arrival in Philadelphia, that piece of information would be a virtually certain clue that his emigration preceded the French and Indian War.

Authenticate the Immigrant Ancestor

The statements in the published Benton County history that David Hite's father (Christopher Hite) was a native of Germany reflect a common source of a misidentified birthplace. There is a marked tendency among people who know (or think they know) their family's country of origin to assume that the first ancestor whose name they know was the immigrant. In the case of David Hite's children, they probably provided the biographical information for the Benton County history themselves. Their grandfather Christopher Hite probably *was* the earliest Hite ancestor whose name they knew. None of them had ever known him personally – David Hite's oldest child was born in 1830, three years after Christopher's death. They did know about his extended Revolutionary War service – an undoubted source of pride to their father. They certainly knew of his German background – all but the youngest were born in Pennsylvania and most of them were old enough to have retained some memory of living in Bedford County and neighboring Blair County prior to the move to Iowa. It is not surprising that late in their lives, their memory of their grandfather's German background gave them the false impression that he had actually been born in Germany – an assertion which, if taken for granted without researching primary sources, could have short-circuited efforts to find his actual background. At least one member of the next generation confused the issue even further. One of David's granddaughters, Jessie Hite Vance (1890-1971) told at least one of her children that David himself had been born in Germany – indicating 19th century immigration for the family. Fortunately, this erroneous statement never found its way into print.

It is worthy of note that this branch of Christopher Hite's descendants, unlike mine, did at least know the correct nationality of their Hite ancestors. I already noted that my father and his siblings grew up with the impression that our Hite ancestors were Dutch. This could, of course, have been a misinterpretation of the term *Pennsylvania Dutch*, but it is also worth noting that the aforementioned history of Benton County was published prior to World War I – before there was any shame in German heritage. At some point after my father and I had proven our lineage back to Christopher Hite, he told me that as a child, knowing nothing beyond the name of his grandfather William Hite, he had an impression that our family went back only one more generation in America – William, he thought, might be the son of someone he described as "a little Dutch boy who got off an immigrant boat" a few years before the Civil War.

The Hites are not my only German ancestors but my great-grandfather, William Henry Albert Hite (1865-1929) appears to have had more German ancestors than any of my other seven great-grandparents. His father, Daniel Hite, Jr. (1832-1882, grandson of the aforementioned Christopher) may have been entirely of German descent – at least, I have yet to find an ancestor of his who was of any other ethnic origin. Daniel's wife, Catherine Ann (Thrawls or Thralls) Hite (1832-1917) is of more mixed heritage although family tradition regarding her would have had me believe otherwise. My paternal grandmother, who never knew her, gave my dad and me the impression that she had been born in the Netherlands and barely spoke English. Her grandson Fred Makadanz, who we met in 1979, did not corroborate that but did give us the impression that she and her husband were both at least partly of Dutch background which agreed with what my grandfather had always said. When we found her on the 1880 census with her husband and children, however, her birthplace was given as Ohio. Once we learned her maiden name, we found her in the 1850 census of Harrison County, Ohio in the household of her father, Samuel Thrawls, who was born in 1809 in Pennsylvania. It was obvious that

Catherine's mother had died by that time because Samuel's wife Sarah was only twenty-five years old, seven years older than Catherine. We later found the record of the marriage of Samuel Thrawls to Sarah Huff in 1845, thirteen years after Catherine's birth. We wanted to know the name of Catherine's mother, so we ordered a copy of her death certificate.

Again – Beware of Death Certificates!

When the certificate arrived, we got a firsthand example of why some items on death certificates must be considered oral history. Her mother's name was simply listed as "not known" which was disappointing but not surprising, given that the informant (Catherine's son Simon Wesley Hite) could never have known his maternal grandmother. Even if a name had been given in the "maiden name of mother slot" on the death certificate, however, I would not have trusted it because the other information on the document was badly garbled. Wesley had identified his maternal grandfather as John Thrawl and indicated that he had been born in Germany. I already knew that Catherine's father was named Samuel Thrawls and that he had been born in Pennsylvania. The lack of an "s" on the end of the surname did not surprise me – many of the later male-line descendants dropped the "s". The incorrect name and birthplace for Catherine's father, however, showed me how little Wesley Hite had known of his heritage. From the beginning I had suspected that whatever alleged Dutch heritage Catherine may have had was actually German and the information on this death certificate – issued, incidentally, about six weeks before the United States entry into World War I – strengthened the case for that. Aside from that, it was utterly useless for furthering knowledge of her background. It was fortunate that Catherine's death certificate was not the first source I checked when researching her ancestry.

This death certificate is also another example of someone assuming that the earliest ancestor they know about is the immigrant ancestor. Wesley Hite had obviously known that his mother was at least partly of German descent and jumped to the conclusion that her father had been from Germany – even though he did not know the correct name of her father. In some respects it is surprising that he did not know Samuel Thrawls's name. Wesley was born in 1861 and Samuel did not die until 1877. However, Wesley left Ohio with his parents before he was even three years old and may not have ever seen his grandfather again after that time. Had Catherine, her husband, and her children remained in Ohio, the children probably would have known more about the background of both of their parents.

Eventually, I did locate a record of Samuels Thrawls's first marriage – to Elizabeth Huff, a sister of his second wife. I have yet to identify Samuel's parents, though circumstantial evidence strongly suggests that he was a descendant of Richard Thralls who lived in Prince George County, Maryland for much of his adult life and died in Washington County, Maryland in 1798. Richard was almost certainly of English origin and, if not born in America, was certainly in the country by the time of the American Revolution which some of his sons served in. Samuel's wife Elizabeth Huff was born in 1813 in Somerset County, Pennsylvania and her father and grandfather were both named Thomas Huff. This family also appears to be of English origin with roots in Kent County, Maryland. So by now, I am sure everyone is wondering where Catherine's German lineage came from. Her maternal grandmother, Mary (Hiestand) Huff, born in the 1780s in Montgomery County, Pennsylvania, was a descendant of German immigrants although her paternal ancestors had been in America for quite some time – her great-grandfather, Abraham Hiestand, is known to have been in Pennsylvania by 1726. Even in this case, the Hiestand family cannot really be properly identified as German – they were descendants of Mennonites who left Switzerland for Germany by 1662 according to the research of Kent D. Hiestand of Colorado, who is preparing a book on the family and is the foremost authority on their origins. So Catherine Ann (Thrawls) Hite, far from being an immigrant or the daughter of immigrants, was a descendant of families that had established themselves in the American colonies prior to the War of Independence. The "oral history" information obtained from her death certificate was all but useless in determining her ancestry. I was fortunate in that I had already identified her father and his birthplace by the time I found it so it did not lead me astray.

In some cases, however, the "oral history" portion of primary sources can be more helpful. In 1986, my dad and I located the estate record of Christopher Hite of Bedford County, Pennsylvania who had died in 1827. This document proved what I already suspected – he was the father of my then-earliest known Hite ancestor, Daniel Hite (1797-1872) who had been born in Pennsylvania and relocated to Tuscarawas County, Ohio about 1825. The document listed Christopher's other heirs also and I hoped to find one who had lived long enough to be enumerated on the 1880 census. That census is critical because it is the first one that asked for the birthplaces of parents. These birthplaces demand verification – they are another items in a source generally regarded as primary that must be viewed as "written oral history". They are, nonetheless, useful clues. I was convinced then (and still am) that Christopher and his wife Margaret were both born in Pennsylvania but I wanted further evidence of that. The name of one of the heirs, Jacob Wisel, led me to that source. It was obvious Jacob was a son-in-law of Christopher and Margaret. I did not know the name of the daughter he had married but I knew I could find out if they had lived until at least 1850.

The 1850 census of Bedford County did, indeed, list Jacob Weisel, aged 52, and his wife Mary, aged 45. This placed Mary's birth as approximately 1805, which was in the age range I expected. Before moving on to later census records, I checked some published volumes of Bedford County cemeteries. I struck paydirt immediately. Jacob and Mary were listed in a cemetery in the small town of Imler, Pennsylvania – a cemetery I had visited before – and they were buried right next to Samuel Hite (1810-1876) who I already knew to be a son of Christopher Hite. It was now obvious that this Mary Weisel was Christopher Hite's daughter. More importantly, the listing indicated that she had not died until 1886. Seeing that, I went directly to the 1880 census of Bedford County. She and Jacob, who had lived until 1883, were both still there. Mary's record, however, did not give the birthplaces of her parents as Pennsylvania. Instead, it indicated that both of her parents were born in Baden.

It Was Wrong – But it Led to What was Right

I was immediately skeptical of this. I knew that Baden was a specific region of Germany, but I also knew that Christopher Hite had been born about 1759. I had no documentation of his birthplace, but I knew that a brother of his - Conrad Hite (1763-1835) - had given Bedford, Pennsylvania as his own birthplace on his Revolutionary War pension application. At the time, I was not certain that Conrad was Christopher's brother, but I suspected the connection. As previously noted, I also knew that emigration from Germany to the American colonies had ground to a halt during the French and Indian War, which raged from the mid-1750s until 1763. Nonetheless, I thought it was a very real possibility that this mention of Baden might be an important clue to the family's origin.

Armed with this clue, I turned to the International Genealogical Index to search for Heyd families in Baden. I found a few in the early 18th century with given names that had been used by the first generations of my Hite family in Pennsylvania. There was a Conrad Heyd listed in the records of the village of Richen. The village of Meckesheim listed a few men named Christoph Heyd and this became even more interesting when I learned that a son of one of these Christoph Heyds (Valentine Heyd, born 1807) had come to America before 1850 and settled in Benton County, Iowa, the same county that Christopher Hite's son David had taken up residence in. It was not long, though, before I honed in on the village of Grötzingen, just east of the city of Karlsruhe, as the most likely place of origin of my family. Some of the given names they commonly used for male members of the family – Christoph, Jacob, Georg, and David – had all been utilized by my ancestors in the late 18th century. A 1787 tax record for Bedford County gave the occupation of John Hite (the father of Christopher and Conrad Hite) as "baker." A Johannes Heyd, who had married in Grötzingen in 1738, was also identified on his marriage record as a baker – and there had been no further mention of him in the village's church records. It took a DNA test to confirm the connection, but I now know that Grötzingen is the ancestral home of my Hite family. Christopher Hite was a native Pennsylvanian – his father John was almost certainly the immigrant Johannes Heyt who arrived in Philadelphia aboard the ship *Shirley* on 5 September 1751, about eight years before Christopher's birth, and there is no baptismal record for Christopher in Grötzingen. The false birthplace information for Christopher, provided by his daughter on the 1880 census, gave me the first clue that led me down that path to my ancestors' German village of origin. Thank you, Great-Great-Great-Great-Aunt Mary, for getting that one wrong!

How Far Away I Could Have Strayed

The falsely identified birthplaces of my various ancestors, provided verbally or in writing in various sources, have ranged from being totally meaningless (like the allegation that my great-grandfather Hite was born in Bloomington, Indiana) to incredibly productive (like the false statement that Christopher Hite was born in Baden). My experiences have taught me how important it is to document these oral statements of birthplaces and learn what I can from them, even when they are not correct for the person

54

Figure 2 - This page of the 1880 census of King Township, Bedford County, Pennsylvania, lists Mary Hite Wisel, age 75, on line 8. The birthplace given for her parents (Baden) is not correct, but this entry did suggest that there might be family origins in Baden. This was the first clue that led to the eventual discovery of the birthplace of Mary's grandfather, John Hite (Johannes Heytt), in the village of Grötzingen in what was then the Margravite of Baden-Durlach in modern-day Germany.

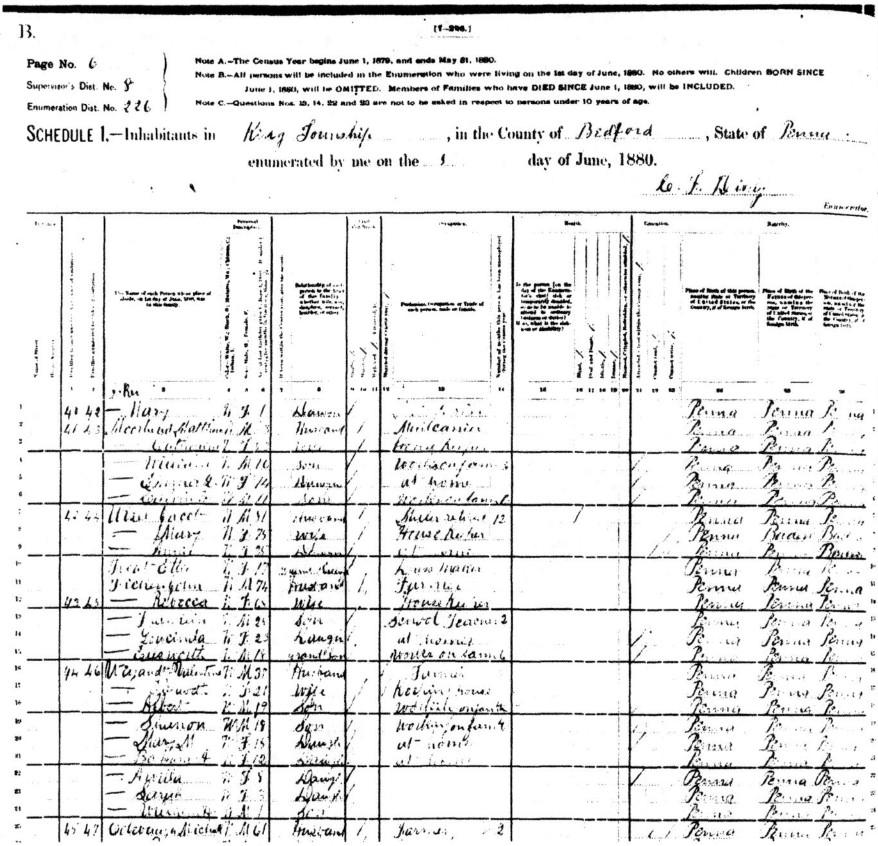
B.

Page No. 6
Supervisor's Dist. No. 8
Enumeration Dist. No. 226

Note A.—The Census Year begins June 1, 1879, and ends May 31, 1880.
Note B.—All persons will be included in the Enumeration who were living on the 1st day of June, 1880. No others will. Children BORN SINCE June 1, 1880, will be OMITTED. Members of Families who have DIED SINCE June 1, 1880, will be INCLUDED.
Note C.—Questions Nos. 13, 14, 22 and 23 are not to be asked in respect to persons under 10 years of age.

SCHEDULE 1.—Inhabitants in King Township, in the County of Bedford, State of Penna, enumerated by me on the 1 day of June, 1880.

they are associated with. Had my father not been with me to calm my youthful exuberance that summer in the Bloomington Public Library, I might have traced William Hite (born 1869 near Bloomington) back to his great-great-grandfather Thomas Hight (born 1757 in Charlotte County, Virginia) a Revolutionary War soldier of English descent and falsely claimed him as an ancestor. By the same token, had I not been skeptical of the census record that gave Christopher Hite's birthplace as Baden, I might have hired a professional genealogist to conduct a village-by-village search of baptismal records from 1757 to 1761 looking for a Christoph Heyd with a father named Johannes. Because I was more careful (or, to be fair, my father was more careful the first time) I eventually discounted the Indiana census record and I knew enough not to take Mary Hite Weisel's Baden claim for granted. Because of this, I did not latch on to the wrong Hite ancestors and I eventually found the right ones. To be successful, all genealogists must exercise similar care when reviewing alleged birthplaces of ancestors provided by oral history, be it "truly oral" or "written oral history."

Chapter 7 - Military Service of Ancestors

When I hear of some of the wildly exaggerated claims of the military exploits of my own ancestors and anyone else's, I am reminded of "The Battle of Mayberry" episode of the *Andy Griffith Show*. In one episode, Opie's class was assigned to write an essay about the so-called "Battle of Mayberry" which had involved the early settlers of the town of Mayberry and the Native American population two centuries earlier. Andy and Aunt Bea immediately told Opie about his own ancestor, Colonel Carlton Taylor who, by their account, played a leading role in the battle. Opie then went on to talk to all of the major characters in the town (Clara Edwards, Floyd the barber, Goober Pyle) and all told stories about ancestors who held the rank of "Colonel" at the time of the battle. All of them described the settlers winning the battle with only fifty armed men facing 500 Native Americans. Andy, realizing Opie's confusion over the conflicting accounts, took him to visit a local Native American named Tom Strongbow who told a completely different story of his own ancestor, Chief Strongbow, leading fifty warriors to a victory over 500 armed settlers. This, of course, confused Opie even further. Finally, Andy took Opie to Raleigh, North Carolina, the state capital, to give him an opportunity to look up contemporary accounts of the battle. What Opie found was a newspaper account that told of a dispute that started over a cow accidentally killed by a Native American in Mayberry. Instead of fighting a battle though, fifty settlers and fifty braves settled the dispute by sharing several jugs of liquor and killing some deer to compensate the owner of the cow.

From Private to Major

That whole story is, of course, fictitious but exaggerated accounts of ancestors' military exploits are a dime a dozen in oral history whether "truly oral" or "written oral." One of the most common mistakes is an inflated rank assigned to an ancestor. A likely source of this, particularly for Civil War soldiers, stems from the late 19th and early 20th century habit of referring to elderly veterans of that war as "Colonel" or "Major" – even for those that never rose above the rank of private. This was most common for Confederate veterans, but Union veterans were also referred to by these honorary titles in some instances. It is easy for overeager descendants who hear an ancestor referred to by an honorary rank to jump to the conclusion that he actually did hold such a rank while in the service. Usually, these claims of such high rank are relatively easy to check, especially for Civil War soldiers. Records for soldiers in earlier wars are not so voluminous but there are many, nonetheless. Service records and pension applications give the ranks soldiers achieved and it is not at all unusual to learn that an honorary major never actually rose above the rank of private. In the case of common names, proof (or disproof) may be a bit more of a challenge. A descendant of a private named John Smith will undoubtedly have little trouble finding a colonel or a major with that rank in some regiment from the state their own ancestor served from. In this kind of a case, researchers should examine the economic circumstances of the ancestors, before and after the war. Assuming that a man named John Smith, who owned less than fifty dollars' worth of real estate at the time of the 1860 and 1870 census enumerations held the rank of "Colonel" during the Civil War is not a leap of faith I would make.

The General's Right Hand Man...

Sometimes the stories of ancestral military exploits are more specific than an overinflated rank. One of the Pennsylvania German families I descend from is a family named Ickes. In the late 1990s, I was searching for information on them on Genforum.com, which was the primary means of exchanging genealogical information on the Internet at the time. I came across an account posted by a descendant of Nicholas Ickes (1764-1848), the founder of the town of Ickesburg in Perry County, Pennsylvania. Nicholas is not a direct ancestor of mine, but he is related. This descendant noted a family story (which she expressed skepticism about) that Nicholas Ickes had been a right hand man to George Washington and had looked between the logs of the General's cabin to see him kneeling in prayer before a battle.

...Who Only Served Two Months!

This is, of course, a spectacular story. Another family member, however, replied to this message less than a month later. Quoting from Ickes's pension application, she noted that in September 1781, he enlisted in the Continental Army as a substitute for a man named George Evans and marched from Philadelphia County (where he then resided) to Uniontown in Bucks County, Pennsylvania where he was stationed in the garrison and served about two months. His pension application was, in fact, rejected because he did not serve six months.

Clearly the contrast between tradition and documentation here could not be much more stark. The idea that a private who served in the Continental Army for two months became a right hand man to George Washington screams exaggeration. In fact, at the time Nicholas Ickes enlisted in Pennsylvania, Washington was in Yorktown, Virginia, preparing for the siege that became the climactic battle of the war. While Washington did spend the winter of 1781-1782 in Philadelphia, dealing with administrative matters relating to the Continental Army, he was not with the army and so the chances that Nicholas Ickes personally encountered him are virtually nil – and he certainly did not cross the General's path just before a battle. The original poster followed up with a less dramatic version of the original story – a tradition that Nicholas Ickes, while on duty near Washington's headquarters at Valley Forge, peeped through an opening between the boards and saw the General alone on his knees in prayer. This story, while omitting the tradition that Ickes had been a right hand man to Washington, is no more believable. The Continental Army spent the winter of 1777-1778 at Valley Forge and Nicholas Ickes did not enlist until September 1781.

The romanticized story of Nicholas Ickes's Revolutionary War exploits is an easy one to disprove. Some stories are not so easy to prove or disprove. Pension records, land warrant records, and service records are the key sources for learning of the specific unit an ancestor participated in. Upon being told of an ancestor's exploits in a specific battle, the next step is to determine if the ancestor's unit participated in the battle in question. A book published in 1907, *History of Cambria County, Pennsylvania* by Henry Wilson

Storey, contains an erroneous account of the Revolutionary War service of one of my ancestors. The book, which contains genealogical memoirs, includes an account of Amos D. Strong (1863-1915) of South Fork, Pennsylvania, whose wife Lucy Ann Hite (1863-1937) was a second cousin of my great-grandfather William Henry Albert Hite. Storey's account of Lucy's ancestry indicates that she was a daughter of John B. Hite who was born in 1824 in Bedford County (which is true). The account further notes that John B. Hite's father was John Hite, a farmer in Bedford County (which is also true except that the area of Bedford County where the elder John lived became part of the newly-created county of Blair in 1846). Storey's next statement about the family contains serious errors, however. He states that the elder John Hite was a son of "Jacob Hite, a revolutionary soldier who served under Mad Anthony Wayne and rendered good service at the battle of Stony Point."[5]

Suspicious Sign – Wrong Given Name

First of all, the elder John's father was not named Jacob. His name was Christopher. Secondly, the regiment he served in at the time of the battle of Stony Point – Colonel Oliver Spencer's Additional Regiment – did not participate in that battle. Instead, at the time of Stony Point, Spencer's Regiment was with General John Sullivan in the campaign against the Iroquois in upstate New York, essentially engaging in a "scorched earth" policy of destroying the tribe's villages and crops. It is true that later in the war, Christopher Hite *did* serve under Anthony Wayne. Spencer's Regiment, which consisted primarily of New Jersey residents, disbanded in January 1781 and the Pennsylvanians in the regiment were assigned to the Pennsylvania Line which Wayne commanded. Hite was under Wayne's command during the siege of Yorktown and for the rest of the war. It is easy to understand how this story of Christopher Hite's service became misconstrued. The family undoubtedly knew that he had served under Anthony Wayne at some point and the battle of Stony Point – a nighttime seizure of a British fortification at bayonet point - was Wayne's greatest claim to fame during the Revolutionary War. That statement of the Hite ancestor's service in that specific battle may not have even come from the family – the author may simply have taken the statement that he had served under Wayne and made the leap of faith that he had been at Stony Point.

Like so many other stories, one can easily understand the misinterpretation of this one by knowing who knew who in the lineage. Lucy Hite Strong may have been the source of the information. She did not know her paternal grandfather, who died in 1859, four years before her birth. Her father, John B. Hite (born in 1824) might have retained a memory of his grandfather Christopher Hite (who died in 1827) but if so, it would have been very vague. The fact that Christopher was misnamed Jacob in the account would raise questions about its accuracy anyway, even for someone who did not already have detailed information about Christopher Hite's Revolutionary War service. Christopher Hite *did* have a son named Jacob who died relatively young (in his forties in 1837) so if Lucy told the story, she might have simply confused the name of this great-uncle with

---

[5] Henry Wilson Storey, *History of Cambria County, Pennsylvania* (New York, Chicago: Lewis Publishing Company, 1907), Vol. 3, p. 476.

that of her great-grandfather who did, in fact, serve in the Continental Army – but not at Stony Point.

Talk About Wild Goose Chases!

The misinformation in the account of Lucy Hite Strong's background is not hard to disprove with primary source research. Still, one wonders how many of her descendants, or those of her siblings came across this account and searched fruitlessly for an ancestor named Jacob Hite who served under Anthony Wayne in the Continental Army. The only Jacob Hite I know of in the Continental Army was from Virginia rather than Pennsylvania and was not related to Christopher Hite at all. Other Revolutionary War soldiers are harder to document than Christopher Hite. I have another ancestor who was allegedly a militia officer and possibly a Continental Army officer during the war. He was much more affluent than Christopher Hite, being a large landowner in present-day Sampson County, North Carolina, and that should make him easier to trace. The problem in documenting his service stems from his name – John Williams.

Too Common a Name

The stories about this John Williams, who was apparently born in the early 1740s and died about 1799 in Sampson County, are many. Some were printed in newspaper accounts in the 1920s and others appeared in a county history published in 1983 titled *The Heritage of Sampson County.* Williams lived in the area near the border of the present-day townships of Dismal and Little Coharie and a letter to the editor of the *Sampson Democrat* (a newspaper published in Clinton, North Carolina) written by a teacher named John Thomas Alderman was printed in the 13 January 1921 issue. The letter gave this account of Williams's exploits:

During the great struggle for American Independence, there were many Tories in the Little Coharie section of the county; many of them were vicious and gave a great deal of trouble. Fortunately for the Whigs and the better class of all citizens the Tories stood in mortal fear and dread of one man especially. He was a soldier in the Continental army, but secured release from duty to look after affairs which threatened destruction to the lives and homes of the patriots.

Capt. John Williams lived not a great way from Hair's Bridge and knew the people as well as the country. He collected a company of men upon whom he could rely; he was known far and wide as a fearless patriot whose presence in any community struck terror to the bands of marauding Tories. With his company of faithful followers he rescued many families and homes which had been marked for pillage and destruction by the Tories. Fifty years ago, there were still living old people who loved to relate the exciting scenes and experiences of those days.

One day a band of Tories had collected in a meadow right near where Salemburg now stands – it is a field owned by Mr. S.A. Howard – and declared they would wash their hands in the blood of Capt. "She" before the close of the week. On account of some impediment of speech Williams was sometimes familiarly known as "Capt. She". A boy hurried to let Williams know of the plot and the place of rendezvous; without a moment's hesitation, after an hour's ride, he and his men surrounded the camp and only one of the Tories escaped.[6]

Obviously, this is quite a story. There may, in fact, be elements of truth in it. There was a John Williams who was a lieutenant in the 2nd North Carolina Regiment of the Continental Line. He enlisted in September 1775 and retired from the army 1 June 1778 which fits with the story that Captain Williams had left the service to attend to affairs in his home community. Other men from the same area are known to have served in the 2nd North Carolina, including another of my own ancestors, Charles Butler (whose granddaughter Sarah Jane Butler married John Williams's grandson John Carouth Williams). With a name like John Williams, however, there is simply not enough evidence to assume that the lieutenant in the 2nd North Carolina is the one from Sampson County.

There is also some evidence that the event with the Tories in the meadow might have elements of truth to it. Two pension applications by soldiers from Sampson County (both named John Register, ironically) mention their participation in a skirmish with Tories near the home of Captain *She* Williams on Cohara (sp, should be Coharie). The applications note that two Tories were killed and some others were wounded and taken prisoner. There is no mention of Captain Williams commanding the men – both applicants noted that they served under a captain named Robert Merritt.

It Could be True, But...

Obviously, no responsible genealogist would publish the 1921 account of Captain John Williams as proven fact. Fortunately John C. Rosser, Jr., who did write a book on this Williams family, reported the story for what it was – oral history. It qualifies as "written oral history" because it appeared in a newspaper account. By the time it was committed to print – 1921 – there had not been any living Revolutionary War soldiers for more than fifty years. Anyone old enough to have even the vaguest memory of the events described could have been born no later than about 1775 and would certainly have been long dead by 1921. The author, John Thomas Alderman, was born in 1853 and grew up in Sampson County so while he may have had some vague childhood memories of people who remembered the Revolutionary War, they could not have been vivid one. Alderman *did* know his maternal grandfather, Thomas Howard (1790-1875) who was a grandson of Captain John Williams and could have remembered the captain, who died about 1799. These facts, combined with the evidence from the Registers' pension applications, suggest that the accounts of John Williams's legendary role in the Revolutionary War are at least partially true – nothing has been found to *disprove* any of it after all as was the case with the accounts about Nicholas Ickes and Christopher (not

---

[6] John Thomas Alderman, letter to the editor, *Sampsonian Democrat,* Clinton, NC, `3 January 1921, reprinted in John C. Rosser, Jr., *Coharie to Cape Fear: The Descendants of John Williams and Katharine Galbreth of Sampson and Cumberland Counties in North Carolina (1740-1990)* , Marceline, MO: Walsworth Publishing Company, 1990, 15-17.

Jacob) Hite. They are not, however, documented well enough to make Captain John "She" Williams a suitable subject for a serious historical biography. They *could* be utilized by an author interested in writing a historical novel about conflicts between Whigs and Tories in Sampson County – but no responsible genealogist will consider such material established as facts. It is only because of the references to Captain "She" Williams in the Registers' pension applications that I feel confident in saying definitively that John "She" Williams served in the Revolutionary War at all.

Did He Serve at All?

That brings up another possibility that genealogists must always consider – a story of an ancestor's service in a particular war may not be true at all. In my own branch of the Hite family, there was no tradition of any service in the Civil War. In fact, when my dad and I began our research, the earliest ancestor we knew about was his aforementioned grandfather, William Henry Albert Hite, who was not born until the Civil War was over. We were quickly able to identify William's father, Daniel Hite, who, born in 1832, would have been a likely age to have served in the war. It was not until we made contact with another descendant of Daniel, a granddaughter of William's oldest brother, John Samuel Hite, that we heard of any tradition that Daniel did serve in the Union Army in that war. This great-granddaughter of Daniel recalled hearing that after his early death (in 1882, which left his wife Catherine with a five year old daughter and several teenagers living at home) his widow and young daughter survived on a Civil War pension. She even recalled hearing of a discussion of who would pay the funeral expenses when Catherine died in 1917 and a statement made by someone to the effect of "Let Wes (Catherine's son) pay 'em, he's been getting her pension for years." There is, indeed, documentation that suggests Catherine may have received a pension of some sort. The 1910 census of Johnson County, Kansas listed her in the household of her son, Elmer Hite (1867-1931). In the column for "occupation" for Catherine the term "own income" was listed. She certainly had not inherited any wealth so it's hard to think of anything other than a pension of some type as a source for that.

Daniel Hite, Jr., however, lived in Tuscarawas County, Ohio, the county he was born in until 1864 when he and his family moved to Tazewell County, Illinois. Extensive searches of the records of Civil War rosters for both states have turned up no one named Daniel Hite (of any conceivable spelling). Pennsylvania records were also searched to see if he had gone there to enlist with his cousins who lived there. Again, nothing was found although he did have a younger cousin who was also named Daniel Hite that served in a Pennsylvania regiment. Indiana records were checked because its location between Ohio and Illinois, but nothing was found. Searches of Civil War pension records also revealed nothing. There is no GAR marker on Daniel's grave in Bella Vista Cemetery in El Dorado, Kansas. He never lived in any state that comprised the Confederacy, so there is no reason to believe he served in the Confederate Army. Ultimately, there is simply no evidence to indicate that Daniel Hite served in the Civil War at all.

So how would one explain the story of Catherine's pension? That has yet to be resolved but given the entry on the 1910 census, it must have some validity. The possibility that she posed as the widow of another Hite who *had* served cannot entirely be ruled out. It is also true that the circumstances of Daniel's early death (15 days shy of his fiftieth birthday) remain unknown. What is known is that he and Catherine sold their farm west of El Dorado in March 1881, twenty months before Daniel's death. Perhaps he went to work in the town (possibly for the railroad or something similar) and was killed on the job somehow. That might have entitled Catherine to a pension. Further research on the matter is clearly needed but the idea that Daniel Hite was a Union veteran of the Civil War can now be discounted.

Through the years, I have located three direct ancestors that did fight in the Civil War. Two great-great-grandfathers, John Webster Bagley (1832-1863) of Pennsylvania and Elijah N. Cook (1847-1872) of Indiana served in the Union Army while Charles T. Grogan (1836-1885) of North Carolina was a Confederate soldier. I only knew of one of them – John Webster Bagley – before I began my research and the story that was told about him (the fact that he died of dysentery while in the service) proved to be true. I knew nothing of the others – in the case of Elijah N. Cook, I did not even know his name which is not surprising since my great-grandmother Emma Catherine Cook was a posthumous child of his and she died in 1921, a year before my grandparents were married. No one I ever met had even known her. In the case of Charles T. Grogan, the paternal grandfather of Melba (Grogan) Williams (1909-1987), I knew his name but neither my grandmother nor any of her sisters knew of his Civil War service. Again, that is not surprising. He died when their father, Thomas Robert Grogan (1867-1946) was in his late teens and to compound that situation, Charles and his wife, Mary Ann (Carter) Grogan (1837-1907) separated when Mary Ann was pregnant with her last child, William Benton Grogan (1871-1956). Thomas may never have seen his father again. I was skeptical of the separation story until I found Mary Ann and all of her children in the 1880 household of her parents, Thomas Carter (1810-1888) and Mary Wray (1806-1886) in Mayo Township of Rockingham County, even though Charles was still alive at that time. He was living alone in Leaksville Township of Rockingham County. So it is not surprising that there was no oral tradition of Charles's service in the Confederate Army. His service was brief. He was conscripted in April 1864 into the 63rd Regiment of the 5th North Carolina Cavalry and was promptly taken prisoner on 7 May 1864 at the battle of Spotsylvania. He was taken to a Union prison at Point Lookout, Maryland and then later transferred to another one in Elmira, New York where he sat out the rest of the war.

Nothing to Joke About

Charles's service was not voluntary and I later found some copies of family letters written in the 1860s. One of them, written by Charles's sister in 1862, noted that Charles had bought a substitute at that time. Knowing that, I very nearly started an undocumented oral tradition myself. In talking about that to my oldest nephew (who was a Civil War re-enactor at the time), I jokingly commented that Charles Grogan probably surrendered to the first guy in a blue uniform he saw at Spotsylvania. Several years later, when we were talking about it again, I realized that he had thought my comment had been a serious one – he had taken it to mean Charles's intentional surrender to a Union soldier was a documented fact. Had I not corrected him, I might have inadvertently created another oral history with no basis in documentation. I realized then that even serious genealogists have to be careful what they joke about. My nephew has children now – they might have passed on the tradition of a flagrant act of cowardice on Charles Grogan's part all because of my joke.

Traditions of heroic (or not so heroic) military service by ancestors are often among the most cherished by family historians. They are interesting because they provide family connections to events well-known by nearly all Americans. They also "flesh out" the stories of military veterans' lives – most genealogists like to know details about how their ancestors lived, not just names, dates, and places – and time spent in the military provides that for certain phases of life in many cases. When I think of my own ancestor, Christopher Hite, who lived from about 1759 until 1827, I realize I know more specifics about how he lived during the six years from 1777 to 1783 than at any other time of his life.

Military service is also one of the facets of genealogical research that is most subject to fabrication by oral history, be it "true oral history" or "written oral history." A man who served two months of guard duty can be transformed by two centuries of storytelling into a right hand man to George Washington. A soldier who was busy destroying Iroquois crops in the summer of 1779 can be portrayed as having stormed the British fortification at Stony Point with a bayonet. A recently-drafted Confederate soldier, thrust into his first battle against hardened three-year veterans, can be inadvertently identified as a coward because of having been taken prisoner in that fight.

As Always, Rely Upon Primary Sources

Military service of ancestors, like all genealogical data, demands verification by primary sources. Primary source research can lead to proving or disproving oral traditions of such service – or, most likely, it will help separate that which is true from that which is not. The best sources are regimental rosters, pension applications, and in the case of the Revolutionary War, land warrant applications. Once regiments are identified, primary sources giving the regiment's history can flesh out the details of an ancestor's military service. When evidence for an ancestor's service is elusive or difficult to confirm (such as in the case of extremely common names like *John Williams*) research on neighbors of the alleged soldiers may prove productive. Such research may also contribute to a conclusion that an ancestor did *not* serve. I carefully reviewed the roster of the 51st Ohio Volunteer Infantry, a regiment comprised heavily of men from Tuscarawas County, Ohio, where Daniel Hite, Jr. lived for most of the Civil War. There was no man named Daniel on the roster with a surname that possibly could have been a corruption of *Hite*. His nephew, Simon Kail, did serve in this regiment and I located a pension application Simon's mother (Daniel Hite's sister) submitted after his death. That, however, contained no mention of any other relatives who served.

The best advice to any genealogist who is looking for information on an ancestor's military service, as with any other genealogical research, is to search the primary sources. Traditions about service *are* worth investigating. Certain facets of these traditions may well be true. However, to assume every detail of these traditions is accurate and not to consider alternative possibilities is a mistake no capable genealogist should ever make.

Postscript: It Was True After All!

Ironically, further research proved that my joke about Charles Grogan having surrendered to the first man in blue uniform he saw has basis in fact – though I had no knowledge of it at the time. His listing on the roll of prisoners of war at Point Lookout, Maryland "desirous to take the Oath of Allegiance to the United States" (prepared obviously by Union troops) notes that Charles "gave himself up to our forces, does not think the South in the right. Wishes to take the oath and go to the Kanawha Valley." This choice of location – the Kanawha Valley in West Virginia – makes sense in light of the fact that two of Charles's brothers already lived in the area. He was not released, however, and was later transferred to Elmira, New York. His entry on the roll of prisoners there "desirous to take the Oath of Allegiance to the United States" in September 1864, notes that he "claims to have been a Union man and to have voted the Union ticket. Gave himself up voluntarily at Todd's Tavern, Spotsylvania County, Virginia".

Whatever Charles Grogan's claim to support the Union cause was based on – his true sympathies or a simple hope to be released from prison and join his brothers in West Virginia – it is clear that he never had any desire to serve in the Confederate Army and chose the quickest path out of the fight at first opportunity. With the war still raging, the Union troops were unlikely to release him unless he agreed to enlist in their army – an option he must have considered less desirable than sitting out the rest of the war in the prison in Elmira. Whether or not he truly was a Union sympathizer, he did return home to North Carolina after the war – not surprisingly, since he had a wife and a young son waiting there for him. Some might dismiss him as a coward. Others might view him as a pragmatist who survived the war by choosing the lesser of two evils every step of the way. In any event, he did survive, though his life after the war was hardly idyllic. He fathered four more children, but his wife eventually took them and left him to return to her parents' home, reportedly because of his persistent drinking and womanizing. As previously noted, the breakup of Charles Grogan's marriage is documented by the 1880 census of Rockingham County, North Carolina, which shows his wife and children living with her parents while Charles lived alone. At that point, he had little time left though. He died at the early age of forty-nine in 1885, allegedly found under the front steps of the very house he was born in, a victim of alcohol poisoning – another oral tradition that remains to be proven.

Figure 3 - Abstract of entry concerning Charles T. Grogan from the "Roll of Prisoners of War at Elmira, New York desirous to take the Oath of Allegiance to the United States." This entry notes that Grogan, conscripted for service in the Confederate Army, gave himself up voluntarily to Union forces at Todd's Tavern in Virginia and that he had always been a Union man and had voted the Union ticket.

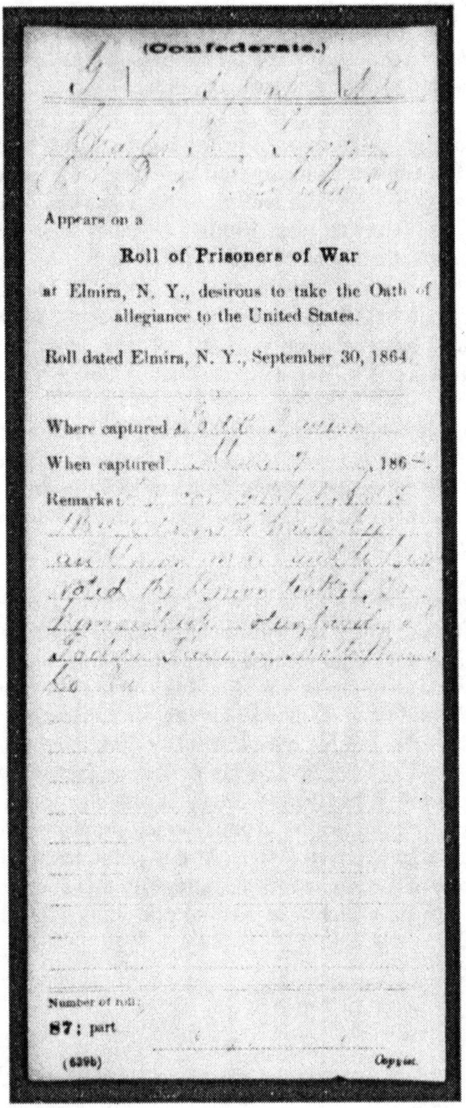

(Confederate.)

Appears on a

Roll of Prisoners of War

at Elmira, N. Y., desirous to take the Oath of allegiance to the United States.

Roll dated Elmira, N. Y., September 30, 1864.

Where captured

When captured , 186

Remarks:

Number of roll:

87; part

(639b)

Copyist.

Chapter 8 - Two or More Brothers as Immigrants

This is a story that is often true. Family after family has a tradition of having been founded in the American colonies (or the United States after the American Revolution) by two or more brothers that emigrated from a specific country of origin. Indeed, it was not unusual for extended family groups, regardless of relationship, to come to the New World together. By the same token, it was also quite commonplace for one individual or nuclear family who immigrated to be followed by next-of-kin within a few years. Usually, groups of related nuclear households that migrated across the ocean settled in close proximity to each other, at least initially. Later, one or member members of the family might move on while others stayed behind.

The problem with this oral tradition is that far too often, researchers have jumped to conclusions that two or more immigrants with the same surname were brothers without any evidence for such a connection. This is often assumed even for two or more such men that never even lived in the same general area. Beginning genealogists who have heard the "two brothers" tradition from a grandparent or another older relative may be too hasty in latching on to two men with the same surname and assuming they were brothers. Often these traditions found their way into print. Family genealogies published in the late 19th and early 20th centuries are teeming with them.

Were They Ever Neighbors?

Even for families in the New England states, the region with the most complete records from the colonial era, published genealogies often identified men with the same surname as brothers without offering any documentation. This sort of material falls into the category of "written oral history" though in many cases it may have originated as "true oral history" or it may have spawned such history. An example from my own lineage is the Ingersoll surname. I descend from John Ingersoll, whose first documented home in New England was Hartford, Connecticut where his presence is recorded in 1653. Two years later, he was in Northampton, Massachusetts and by 1666, he had relocated to Westfield, Massachusetts where he died in 1684. A genealogy of this family was published by Lillian Drake Avery in 1926, which also includes the families of Richard Ingersoll (who settled in Salem, Massachusetts in 1629) and another John Ingersoll, who settled on Long Island by 1654. Instead of treating the families as separate ones, however, the author (without citing any evidence) stated that my ancestor, John Ingersoll (born in 1615 according to her account) accompanied his brother Richard to Salem in 1629 and then lived there for a time before moving to Hartford. She did not identify the birthplace of either Ingersoll in England, nor did she cite any document in Salem records that identified them as brothers. It is far from clear how she reached that conclusion. A tradition of "two brothers as immigrants" may have been all she needed.

How Close in Age Were They?

Subsequent research on John Ingersoll, published in the *New England Historic Genealogical Register,* identified him as having been born in 1626 in Derby in the

English county of Derbyshire, a son of Thomas Ingersoll and Margery Eaton. Long before that, research on Richard Ingersoll had led to documentation of his birth in Edworth, Bedfordshire, England in 1587, son of George Ingersoll. So Richard was nearly forty years older than his alleged brother John. The counties of Derbyshire and Bedfordshire do not adjoin. There is no known record of interaction between the families of John and Richard Ingersoll in 17th century New England and Richard, who died in 1644, was probably dead by the time John arrived in the colonies. The closest John ever lived to Salem, where Richard settled, was more than 100 miles away. Ultimately, there is no reason to think that John and Richard were even related, much less brothers. The tradition of "two brothers" in this case led to false information appearing widely in print for more than seventy years before being dispelled by primary documentation in England.

The Ingersoll "brothers" case illustrates once again how serious scholars of other subjects – even history – are often unaware of the questionable nature of oral history in genealogy, particularly "written" oral history. As recently as 2007, ten years after the publication of information on the English origins of John Ingersoll, the director of the Robert Green Ingersoll Birthplace in Dresden, New York remained unaware of it. I had occasion to communicate with him and I quickly realized that he still regarded the 1926 work by Lillian Drake Avery as the definitive work on the Ingersoll genealogy. Robert Green Ingersoll (1833-1899) was a noted attorney and agnostic orator of the late 19th century and was a descendant of Richard Ingersoll, my ancestor John's alleged brother. The article on John's English origins also included a transcription of a bout of spiritual turmoil he experienced when he was in his thirties, one that nearly drove him to suicide. The museum director Thomas Flynn (who is also the editor of the magazine *Free Inquiry* and certainly an accomplished scholar) still regarded John Ingersoll as an uncle, several generations removed, of Robert Green Ingersoll and remarked on the irony that the leading nineteenth-century proponent of free thought in America had an indirect ancestor who suffered through such a traumatic spiritual crisis. I took no pleasure in pointing out the inaccuracy of that alleged genealogical connection, knowing that it burst his bubble and also because I would have found it equally ironic had it been true. But to me, Robert Green Ingersoll is no more than a famous person who just happened to have the same surname as some of my ancestors.

A similar tradition of two immigrant brothers has been published involving another of my New England ancestral families – Hoyt. I am a descendant of Simon Hoyt, born in West Hatch, Somerset, England in 1593, who arrived in Salem, Massachusetts in 1628 with his family. He was quite a wanderer, relocating to Dorchester, Massachusetts by 1630, Scituate, Massachusetts in 1635, Windsor, Connecticut in 1639, Fairfield, Connecticut by 1649, and finally to Stamford, Connecticut where he died in 1657. Simon was not the only Hoyt to arrive in Massachusetts in the first half of the 17th century. By 1640, there was a John Hoyt living in Salisbury, Massachusetts who became one of the original proprietors of the newly-created town of Amesbury in 1654. Less peripatetic than Simon, John lived the rest of his life in Amesbury, dying there in 1688.

It's in the DNA

As with the Ingersolls, printed sources have often identified Simon and John as brothers. Like Richard and John Ingersoll, the two men appear to be separated by a generation in age. John's birthdate is not known, but his oldest children were born in the late 1630s, which suggests a year of birth for him in the 1610s – perhaps only slightly before the births of Simon's oldest known children. John's English birthplace has not been identified which, in and of itself, is a clue that he was not Simon's brother given that Simon has been located in English vital records. Unlike the Ingersolls, however, a relationship has not been *disproven* (or at least proven unlikely) by original sources. This, however, is a case that has been solved by DNA. No fewer than fourteen identifiable descendants of Simon Hoyt have taken the DNA test and six descendants of John have participated in the testing. As one would expect, the descendants of Simon match each other as do the descendants of John. However, the DNA readings for Simon's family are not even remotely similar to those of John's descendants. Clearly, Simon and John Hoyt were not related – even though some written and oral history of the 19th and early 20th century calls them brothers.

The Case of the Missing Brother

Even without DNA evidence, the idea that Simon and John Hoyt were brothers should have been laid to rest with the discovery of Simon's origins in a specific location in England. Had John Hoyt, the settler of Amesbury, been Simon's brother or some other close relation, he should also have been found in the records of West Hatch, Somerset. In cases when two or more brothers actually did immigrate to the New World, finding the European home of one of them is usually all it takes to find the others. With names like Simon and John, the given name Simon is far less common and so the chances of finding him in European records were far better. However, once he *was* located, it should have been easy to determine if he had a brother (or perhaps a nephew) named John Hoyt who also sailed to America. No such person was found in the records in or near West Hatch so that would have dashed the idea that the two men were brothers even without the DNA results. It did not take DNA testing to prove that Richard and John Ingesoll were not brothers – both were found in different English counties – but in the absence of other evidence, DNA is always a useful tool.

Would 5th Cousins Really Resemble Each Other?

The assumption that two early immigrants with the same surname were brothers is not limited to those who settled in the same general region. As an example, there were two large families in the American colonies with the surname Cleveland – one in New England and one in Virginia. The New England Clevelands descend from Moses Cleveland who settled in Woburn, Massachusetts by 1642 and died there in 1702. President Grover Cleveland and a later Moses Cleveland (the founder of Cleveland, Ohio) both descend from him. The Virginia family descends from Alexander Cleveland, born about 1659, who lived in Prince William County, Virginia whose father (probably named Alexander or Roger) may have remained in England or may also have come to

Virginia. A Cleveland family genealogy, published in 1899, examines both of these families and offers the conjecture (without citing any documentation) that Moses and the father of Alexander were brothers (the book gives Alexander as the definitive name of the father of the younger Alexander, it is other sources that give Roger as an alternative possibility). This conjecture can only be based on oral tradition. The book cites a strong physical resemblance between members of the two families. However, the very oldest members of each family, living in 1899, must have been born no earlier than the very early 19th century – about five generations beyond Alexander and six beyond Moses. If Alexander was Moses's nephew, any living descendants by the time of the publication of the book were probably no more closely related than fifth cousins – meaning that at most, they would have shared one out of thirty-two sets of great-great-great-great-grandparents. Any physical resemblance between relatives that distant can generally be written off as coincidental or the product of an overactive imagination on the part of the observers.

This is not to say that it is impossible that the two Cleveland families were related. DNA testing has not yet proven otherwise, though it does hint that there is no relationship (some southern Clevelands, without documentation of a lineage to Alexander, have taken the test and have not matched the descendants of Moses). It does seem likely, however, that if the two immigrant ancestors were brothers or closely related, they would have settled near each other, at least initially. There appears to be no record of contact in the colonies between the two families so the assumption of such a relationship appears to be just that – an assumption.

Coincidental Arrivals

Another source of the tradition of two or more immigrant brothers may arise simply from the fact that two or more men with the same surname arrived in the colonies around the same time. That situation is exacerbated if one of the men became particularly noteworthy. As an example, the 1710 migration of Germans to New York (after a year in England) included three men with the surname Heyd. One of them, of course, was Hans Justus Heyd, whose name was anglicized to *Jost Hite* by the time he took up residence in Virginia's Shenandoah Valley and played a leading role in its settlement. Many secondary sources on Jost Hite identified him as a native of the Alsace-Lorraine region of present-day France until his baptismal and marriage records (1685 and 1704 respectively) were located in his native village of Bonfeld in the Kraichgau region of Germany. The other two Heyd men in that group were definitely not related to Jost. Peter Heyd, who remained in New York for about a decade before returning to Germany, was a native of the town of Baumholder in the present-day Rheinland-Pfalz – quite a distance from the Kraichgau. The other 1710 Heyd immigrant was Nicolaus Heyd, who may or may not have been Peter's brother (Peter did have a brother named Nicolaus, but it is not proven or disproven that he was the 1710 immigrant). Nicolaus settled in or near Somerville, New Jersey and had children baptized in the Reformed Church there in the 1710s.

Even though neither Peter nor Nicolaus Heyd was related to Jost Hite (and even though Jost Hite was not from the Alsace-Lorraine region), this immigration has created false oral traditions. In the late 1990s and early 2000s, descendants of a New Jersey Hight family posted messages on the website Genforum.com that noted the arrival of three brothers as immigrants from Alsace-Lorraine sometime before the Revolutionary War. One had supposedly settled in New York (obviously Peter), one in Virginia (an obvious reference to Jost Hite), and one in New Jersey (obviously Nicolaus). Here was an oral tradition of three brothers as immigrants based solely on the arrival of three men with the same surname in the same large group of arrivals in the colonies.

Are They Even from the Same Country?

Clearly, this New Jersey Hight family was not related to Jost Hite of Virginia and DNA testing subsequently proved this. The family could be descended from Nicolaus Heyd, but that also seems unlikely based on DNA evidence and other facts about where they lived. Peter Heyd, as previously noted, returned to Germany but his cousin Conrad Heyd came to the country later, arriving in Philadelphia in 1738. Some of Conrad's documented descendants have taken the DNA test and their results did not match those of the New Jersey Hights. Therefore, if Peter and Nicolaus were brothers, Nicolaus cannot be the ancestor of the New Jersey Hights. Even if that relationship (Nicolaus and Peter as brothers) is not correct, the New Jersey Hights are far more likely to be of English origin. They were concentrated in the counties of Middlesex, Somerset, and Mercer and records of the people they interacted with there in the colonial era suggest that their neighbors were primarily of English origin. At one time it was thought they might be descendants of the aforementioned Simon Hoyt (some of whose descendants' surname evolved into *Hight* or *Haight*) but DNA tests eliminated that possibility. The search for the immigrant ancestor (probably an Englishman) of these New Jersey Hights continues.

When Brothers *Did* Emigrate Together

None of the preceding examples are intended to imply that no American families were founded by two or more immigrant brothers. In fact, such a scenario was quite common. Close relatives often did emigrate together or some who initially remained in Europe might follow family members to America later. Examples of brothers that emigrated together or followed each other abound in New England records of the colonial era. Again, I can find examples of this in my own lineage. Two Emery brothers, John (my ancestor, born in 1599) and Anthony (born in 1601), came to Massachusetts from the English village of Romsey, Hampshire, on the ship *James* in 1635 and both initially settled in the town of Newbury, a town of numerous ancestral connections for me. John remained in Newbury the rest of his life, dying there in 1683, but Anthony, who converted to Quakerism, moved around quite a bit – to Dover, New Hampshire in 1640, Kittery, Maine by 1651, and then to Portsmouth, Rhode Island by 1660. It is noteworthy that even though these brothers did not remain as neighbors in the New World, they *did* initially settle in the same town. The same was true of the Treadwell brothers, Thomas (my ancestor, born 1603) and Edward (born 1607) of Epwell, Oxfordshire, in England. Thomas came to Massachusetts in 1635 and, after a brief stop in the town of Dorchester, settled in Ipswich by 1637. Edward does not appear to have sailed with Thomas but he apparently followed soon after, having been noted in Ipswich records in 1637 also. Once again, the two brothers did not stay together. Thomas never lived anywhere in the colonies but Dorchester and Ipswich, but Edward relocated to Long Island by 1649, living in several different towns there before dying in Huntington in 1660 or 1661.

Both of the aforementioned sets of brothers, even though they did not remain in the same communities for the rest of their lives, did settle in close proximity to each other upon first arriving in the American colonies. Even before English records proved they were brothers, this fact alone gave their descendants reason to suspect that they were. Neither Emery nor Treadwell is a particularly common surname, so when two men with those surnames settled near each other soon after arriving in the New World, there was definite reason to suspect they were brothers or closely related somehow. In the cases of the Ingersolls, Hoyts, and Clevelands, however, the pairs of immigrants never lived in close proximity to each other in America. Richard Ingersoll settled in Salem and lived the rest of his life there. His English village of origin was discovered before that of John Ingersoll, who settled first in Hartford, Connecticut before moving on. Luckily for John's descendants, other researchers persisted in the search for his English origins and did not take it for granted that he was from the same village as Richard (despite the written oral tradition that they were brothers). That is where the danger lies in assuming that immigrants of the same surname are brothers or close relatives. Once the place of origin in Europe for one is located, overeager descendants of the other one can find themselves jumping to the hasty conclusion that the same location is their ancestor's place of origin as well. That can stifle research that has the potential to lead to the immigrant ancestor's actual place of origin. Finding the European village or town of origin is always one of the major goals of any American genealogist of European background.

In this day of DNA testing, of course, there are easy ways to prove or disprove that two immigrants with the same surname are related or not. If one can track down direct male line descendants of both – preferably at least two descendants of each immigrant, as distantly related to each other as possible – one can readily find out if the two immigrants have matching Y-chromosomes. Finding a match between the two does not, of course, prove that they are brothers – it simply proves they have a common direct male line ancestor at some point in the past. A non-match proves that there is no relationship as DNA testing on descendants of the New England settlers Simon and John Hoyt has shown.

How Common is the Surname?

When the place of origin of one alleged brother among two or more immigrants with the same surname is discovered in Europe (or wherever) descendants of the others should certainly search the area's records for mentions of their own ancestors (unless the alleged connection has been disproven by DNA tests). This is particularly true for surnames that are not very common – and Ingersoll, Treadwell, and Emery fit that category. For more common surnames like Smith and Brown, researchers have to be particularly careful – it is far too easy to find a John Smith or William Brown anywhere and jump to a hasty conclusion. Ultimately, for surnames that common, Y-chromosome

DNA testing often offers the only true solution. With common surnames, the settlement of two or more men with the same surname in close proximity to each is not such a strong indicator of a close relationship. No fewer than three immigrants with the Brown surname settled in the Massachusetts town of Newbury in the 17th century, including another of my own forbearers - Richard Brown, who arrived on the ship *Mary and John* in 1634 and settled in Newbury by 1638. Richard's grandson, Joseph Brown (1669-1732) married Sarah Treadwell (born 1674), a granddaughter of the aforementioned Thomas Treadwell. Another Brown (Thomas Brown) who arrived a year later on the ship *James* (the same ship as John and Anthony Emery) was documented in Newbury in 1641. Later, in 1651, a James Brown first appeared in the town's records. Richard and Thomas both lived out their lives in Newbury, dying there in 1661 and 1687 respectively. James left for Salem by 1664 and died there in 1676. Despite the fact that all of them settled in the same town, there is no indication that they were related. Because of the commonness of the surname, locating them in England is very difficult, especially in the case of James whose specific arrival date in the colony is not known. The three men could be brothers or cousins, but DNA testing is probably the only way to prove or disprove it. I know of no tradition that these three men were brothers, but it would not surprise me if I ran across a reference that they were at some point - and it is not impossible. If I ever did find a source that indicated that the three Browns in Newbury (or any two of them) were brothers, I would scrutinize it carefully. Even if one of them was positively identified in the records of an English village (say Richard for example) and if the records proved he had a brother named Thomas, I would want to dig deeper before taking it for granted that it was the same Thomas Brown who came to Newbury a few years after Richard.

Of all of the common oral traditions considered, the idea of descent from two or more immigrant brothers is the one that is most likely to be accurate. The risk researchers should avoid is assuming this story is true without documenting it. Even when the story *is* true – as it often is – the actual brother of the immigrant ancestor can be confused with another immigrant with the same surname (or even another one with the same given name). As with all other oral history, assuming it is accurate without verifying it can prevent genealogists from learning their true origins.

Chapter 9 - Associations or Encounters With Famous People

It is a story I heard many times when I was growing up. My great-grandfather, William Henry Albert "Will" Hite was a deputy United States marshal during the Oklahoma Land Rush. While serving in this capacity, he and other deputy marshals chaperoned a dance somewhere near the Kansas-Oklahoma border. Cole Younger, the famous outlaw, and his associates arrived on horseback and demanded to be invited to join the dance. When the marshals told them no, they shot out the lights and galloped away into the night.

Is it Even Chronologically Possible?

I knew of Cole Younger, his outlaw brothers, and their earlier association with Jesse James from having taken an interest in the Old West as a child so this story made quite an impression on me. As my interest in my own family's history grew, I decided to check for more details about this tale. It did not take long for me to learn the impossibility of it. The Oklahoma Land Rush occurred in 1890. By that time, Cole Younger had been in prison for fourteen years, having been captured after a failed bank robbery in Northfield, Minnesota in 1876. He was not released from prison until 1901 and he did not resume his lawbreaking career after that.

Half Truths and Pure Fiction

I doubt I will ever learn the exact truth behind that story. Will and some of his siblings *did* live in Chautauqua County, Kansas (which borders Oklahoma) around that time. Will married in that county in 1892, two years after the land rush, so as a single man in his twenties two years earlier, he would have been a prime candidate for such a job. It is very possible that he was a deputy marshal. It is also possible that he did chaperone a dance and that someone who was refused admission shot out the lights and left. Some notorious outlaws who *were* active in that region at the time of the Oklahoma Land Rush were the Dalton Gang (brothers Bob, Grat, and Emmett Dalton) and their associates. Perhaps they were the ones who shot out the lights. It is equally possible that it was some other group of petty criminals who never became famous – just a group of young men out for a good time that one evening. Another possibility that cannot be discounted is that Will Hite simply made up the entire story. The source of this information (for me and my generation anyway) was my paternal grandmother, Jessie (Bagley) Hite, who was Will's daughter-in-law. She was from Jamestown, New York and had never been west of the Mississippi River until she married my grandfather. Will may have simply been trying to impress his northeastern daughter-in-law with tales of the rough-and-tumble west and exaggerating his own role in it.

Oral traditions such as this are not at all unusual. Like others, they demand proof to be accepted. In most cases, taking them for granted without verification is not as damaging to research as the blind acceptance of some other common traditions is. One exception to this would be when such an encounter places an ancestor's residence in a place other than where s/he actually lived. In the case of Will Hite's alleged encounter with Cole Younger and service as a deputy marshal, it does place him in Kansas, near the border with Oklahoma, which is where he did live at the time.

Another branch of this part of my family also has a tradition about an encounter with famous outlaws. Will Hite's oldest brother, John Samuel Hite (1856-1919), actually participated in the Oklahoma Land Rush and ending up settling in Glencoe, Oklahoma. One of his granddaughters – a daughter of John's youngest daughter Amy Lenora (Hite) Reed – recalled hearing that her mother and other family members occasionally saw the Dalton gang ride by on horseback while working in the fields and would lie down to avoid being seen. The Daltons did spend time in Oklahoma and were still active when John and his family first settled there. Amy, however, was not born until 1895 – three years after the Daltons' outlaw career came to a bloody end when they attempted to rob two banks at once in Coffeyville, Kansas. This raid, on 5 October1892, resulted in the deaths of Bob and Grat Dalton and the wounding and imprisonment of their youngest brother Emmett. Clearly, the Daltons were not still riding in Oklahoma in 1895. Amy Hite did have an older sister, Effie (Hite) Giger (1883-1940) and she was certainly old enough to have some memories of the Daltons. Perhaps it was Effie who hid from them in the fields and the next generation mistakenly involved both sisters, who undoubtedly did work in the fields together once Amy was old enough. But the dates show that the story of Amy hiding in the fields from the Daltons cannot be true – just as the story of Cole Younger and associates attempting to force their way into a dance chaperoned by Will Hite cannot be true.

For families that lived west of the Mississippi River in the 19th century, notorious outlaws are very often the subject of stories of family encounters. Members of another Hite family, unrelated to me (descendants of Jost Hite of the Shenandoah Valley) posted information on the Genforum website in 2000 about Ernest Alfred Hite (1882-1956), a native of Kentucky who later lived in Texas. Some of Ernest's descendants recalled that when he was a child, he was in a hayloft with Jesse James and one of his associates when a group of armed men approached. James and his comrade, lying in the hay with Ernest between them, drew their guns but the other men rode away before any shots were fired.

Again – Chronology is Everything

This is another entertaining story of the old west. Once again, however, the chronology does not fit. Ernest Alfred Hite was born 12 August 1882, four months after the death of Jesse James. Ernest's father, Julius F. Hite (born 1852) *did* have two first cousins (Robert Woodson "Wood" Hite and Clarence Browder Hite) that rode with Jesse James late in his lawbreaking career. The family undoubtedly passed that story down to the point that it got distorted enough to involve Ernest, who was not born until after the death of James. This is, like so many such stories, one that has a grain of truth in it. The specific details, however, have been lost in the retelling.

An unfortunate fact about stories such as this – ancestors' encounters with famous people – is that while they can often be disproven, they can rarely be confirmed even if they are true. The preceding examples can be discounted because they are chronologically impossible, but there may be grains of truth in them. Amy Hite Reed could not have hidden in fields to hide from the Dalton gang - she was not born until their career was over – but her sister Effie Hite Giger could have. Will Hite could not have encountered Cole Younger while working as a deputy United States marshal (if that is even true), but he could have encountered the Dalton gang or some other criminals that never rose to prominence. There is no harm in repeating such stories when they cannot be proven false by chronology – after all, the only way to confirm that Will Hite did encounter some criminals while chaperoning a dance would be if it appeared in a newspaper account somewhere which is unlikely. Such stories, unless proven, should always be qualified by a statement such as "This is how Grandpa (or whoever) told it. It may or may not be true."

A fortunate fact about such stories is that they rarely affect the genealogical details about the person involved. The fact that Will Hite could not have encountered Cole Younger does not affect the proven data about when and where he was born, the names of his parents, who he married, and the names and birthdates of his children. He was still my great-grandfather and I still tell that story to younger generations in the family – although I add that the criminal involved could not have been Cole Younger and the whole tale may have been a fabrication. From everything my grandmother told me about Will Hite, it would not surprise me at all if he *did* make up the entire story.

There *Are* Risks Involved

There are, however, potential pitfalls with such stories if one does not already know other facts about the ancestor alleged to have been involved in such an encounter. As I think about Will Hite, I find myself wondering what the Cole Younger story could have prompted if I did not already know his date of birth. Cole Younger's years of criminal activity began in the late 1860s and continued until his capture in 1876. In that time period, he participated in bank and train robberies in Missouri, Kentucky, Iowa, and Minnesota. There were men named William Hite in those states that were old enough to have been deputy marshals during that time. Had I taken the story of the encounter with Cole Younger for granted, I might have mistakenly identified one of those William Hites as my great-grandfather. That could have led me down the wrong genealogical path for years.

Descendants of Ernest Hite – the boy allegedly in the loft with Jesse James – could have made a similar mistake. Had they taken that story for granted and had not known Ernest's birthdate, they might have identified an older Ernest Hite as their ancestor. Just as with my family, such an error could have led them to pursue the ancestry of the wrong Ernest Hite. Examples such as this illustrate why taking family stories of encounters with famous people for granted can sabotage genealogical research.

Not all family traditions of encounters with famous people are as dramatic as the aforementioned ones. Many involve incidents such as ancestors hearing speeches given by Presidents (Abraham Lincoln is perhaps the most common) or other prominent elected officials. Others may involve an ancestor shaking the hand of a prominent official at a specific event or perhaps just seeing the person. There is one such event in my family that *can* be verified (or nearly verified anyway). In 1912, former President Theodore Roosevelt laid the cornerstone of the Mount Tabor Oddfellows Temple in Jamestown, New York. My great-grandparents, Horace and Matilda (Bush) Bagley lived in Jamestown at the time and I have a photo is of the event. Horace Bagley was supposedly in the crowd and my grandmother, Jessie Bagley Hite, pointed him out to me in the picture during her lifetime. No one person in the photo appears large enough that it is possible to identify him or her with any certainty. However, the individual she pointed out to me could certainly be her father, based on other pictures of him I have seen.

When the Evidence Isn't There

Another source of traditions of such encounters is often correlated with military service. The story of Nicholas Ickes peeping through the logs of George Washington's cabin at Valley Forge and seeing him kneeling in prayer (mentioned in the chapter on ancestral military service) is one such story. Other such stories often involve privates meeting famous generals they served under at some point in the war – George Washington in the case of the Revolutionary War, Ulysses S. Grant or Robert E. Lee in the case of the Civil War, or Theodore Roosevelt in the case of the Spanish-American War. Some stories are more specific. Descendants of Isaac Williams (1837-1920) of Sampson County, North Carolina (a brother of my great-great-grandfather, John Williams) recall a tradition that during Isaac's service in the Confederate Army, he cared for General Lee's horse *Traveller* for some of the time. At this point, there is no way to verify or debunk this. It is perhaps noteworthy though that Isaac did not enter the Confederate Army until September of 1864, when he enlisted in the 63rd Regiment of the 5th North Carolina Cavalry. Unless he somehow showed an unusual ability with horses, it seems unlikely that a soldier who enlisted that late in the war would be entrusted with such a responsibility when there were many other long term veterans around who would have had many more opportunities to earn such a position of trust. Unless there is some specific mention of this responsibility in Isaac Williams's service record, there is probably no way to prove it – unless there are Confederate Army records listing the names of soldiers that were assigned such responsibilities.

Stories such as these, whether true or not, add color to genealogy. Generally there is no harm in repeating them to later generations provided it is specified they are not proven, if they are not. The only real risk in repeating unproven stories like these is that they can place ancestors at an incorrect place at an incorrect time and undermine valid genealogical research.

Chapter 10 - Native American Ancestors

Now we come to the mother of all oral traditions – the story of a Native American ancestor. For years, I have joked that if everyone who claimed to have a Native American in his or her lineage actually did, I would have to assume that if I could travel back in time to the American colonies in 1750 (just to choose a year at random) the wife would be a Native American in half of the households I came across. For some reason, the alleged Native American ancestor is almost invariably a woman who married a white man – not the other way around. These women would not be ordinary Native Americans either – all of them would be Indian princesses (even though there was no such thing because Native Americans did not recognize certain families as royal). Furthermore, at least half, and perhaps as many as ninety percent of these Native American wives would be from one specific tribe - Cherokee - regardless of where they lived. The Cherokee tradition recently made news headlines in the U.S. Senate race in Massachusetts when the oral history of such an ancestor in the family of candidate Elizabeth Warren became politically charged.

I realize, of course, that the statement about half of the wives in the United States being Native Americans is a gross exaggeration – one couple living in the colonies in 1750 census could easily have tens of thousands of descendants living today. The statement is simply designed to drive home a point – the number of Americans who are of European descent but who claim to have a Native American ancestor far exceeds believability. Professional historians who have researched European-Native American relations in colonial America have often noted the rarity of intermarriage between colonists and Native Americans. The same is true in the antebellum United States. When those marriages and out-of-wedlock liaisons *did* happen, the resulting children were far more likely to have remained in Native communities than to have grown up in, and been accepted, as members of white society - at least in most of the areas that became the United States. Intermarriage happened far more often in Canada, meaning that Americans of Canadian descent are among the most likely to have had identifiable Native American ancestors. For those whose families have been in the modern-day United States since the time of arrival from Europe, the tradition is far less likely to have any basis in reality.

The Tallest of Tales

Most of the oral traditions cited in previous chapters, even if proven untrue, often have some basis in truth. Incorrect ethnicities assigned to a particular surname, for example, often turn out to be the actual ethnic identity of an earlier female ancestor in the same lineage. Exaggerated military heroism stories often grow out of actual military service that was far less glamorous. But the tradition of a Native American ancestor often turns out to have no meaningful basis in reality at all. In part, this is because of the wide variety of reasons that the tradition can arise – many of which are so flimsy that they leave one mystified at how such a story been so badly garbled.

Oral history that cites Native American ancestry has originated for a number of different reasons – probably enough to fill a book in and of themselves. What follows are some of the most common sources of oral traditions of Native American forbearers –

1. A female ancestor with an unusual first name.
2. Any history of interactions with Native Americans – regardless of the form the interaction took.
3. Political concerns
4. Physical appearance of ancestors – whether in existing photos or the memories of older relatives.
5. A female ancestor whose maiden name proves elusive.
6. A direct ancestor or collateral relative (almost certainly male) who married, or had a liaison, with a Native American *in addition* to his marriage to the mother of his Caucasian children.
7. A substitute for African ancestry.
8. Fiction and popular culture.

Daddy's Little Princess

One of my favorite stories about a tradition of a female Native American ancestor illustrates the unusual first name source of the origin. A professional archivist posted a family story on the Internet that he remembered from his childhood. He noted that he and his siblings had grown up with a tradition that they were descendants of a Cherokee princess named Parasada – an unusual name and the usual link to the Cherokees and the idea of a "princess." He, however, had dispelled that oral history himself when he researched his own ancestry. He did, indeed, find a female ancestor with the given name of Parasadie – very similar, obviously, to the name he had been told – but he found no evidence that she was any race other than Caucasian. He did, however, eventually find an explanation for the "Cherokee princess" tradition in private family papers. Correspondence between Parasadie and her father revealed that his pet name for her was none other than "Princess." The example illustrates as well as any other how flimsy some of the stories that lead to a tradition of a Native American ancestor can be. It is true that this story does have an element of truth in it just like so many other oral traditions – but the leap from "Daddy's little princess" to a "Cherokee princess" is perhaps as drastic a contrast between tradition and reality as I have every encountered.

It is, perhaps, worthwhile to note the probable reason for the frequent assertion that alleged female Native American ancestors were "Indian princesses". One of the few documented cases of a marriage between a colonist and a Native American the resulted in a mixed race family living in colonial British society was that of John Rolfe and Pocahontas in Jamestown, Virginia in 1614. Pocahontas was the daughter of Powhatan, chief of the powerful Powhatan Confederacy that the first English settlers of Jamestown encountered upon arriving in Virginia in 1607. To the English, Powhatan was the equivalent of a king and therefore his daughter was the equivalent of a princess. When Pocahontas traveled to England with her husband and others in 1616, she was presented to the English public as a princess by the Virginia Company. This title carried no weight among her own people, however, and no other Native American women, even if they were the daughters of chiefs, can properly be called "Princess." Traits attributed to Pocahontas – some accurate, some not – became associated with other Native American women as well and also with women assumed to be Native Americans who were not.

An Unusual Name – But *Still* English

Among those traits that *are* true of Pocahontas is that she did marry an Englishman and she did have a child whose descendants lived in white society. Her thousands of descendants can, of course, properly claim Native American ancestry. There are, however, thousands of other descendants of early English settlers in Virginia who claim Native American descent *improperly*. My own lineage includes some 17th and 18th century Virginians of English descent, among them Edward Harris, who died after 1747 in Prince Edward County, survived by his wife Unity and a son named Nathaniel. DNA testing proved that Edward was somehow related to Thomas Harris, who was in Virginia by 1616 and perhaps as early as 1611 – though it is not clear if Edward was a direct descendant of Thomas or not. Some of Edward's descendants also believe that his wife Unity was a Native American. I had never heard of a tradition of Native American lineage in this family, but it is only recently that I was able to prove a connection to Edward and Unity. Unity's maiden name has never been determined and some descendants, based partly on the idea that she had an unusual name, have concluded that she was a Native American. But no one has offered any documentation of the idea and there is nothing to suggest that the name *Unity* had anything to do with Native Americans. Edward and Unity – whoever she was – were apparently married about 1700, probably in Virginia, but it is also possible they emigrated from England.

This is one case when the work of academic historians proves useful. Historian Gary B. Nash, in his seminal work *Red, White, and Black: The Peoples of Early North America* noted that by the conclusion of Bacon's Rebellion in 1675, "only a few Indians remained in the areas of white settlement" while also noting that the wide availability of white women which reduced whatever motivation the English colonists may have had to marry Native women. Governor Alexander Spotswood claimed in 1717 that not a single intermarriage was known in Virginia at that time.[7] While it seems impossible that Spotswood could have known this absolutely, his statement to that effect does suggest that such intermarriages were a rare occurrence. Spotswood was not speaking of this lack of intermarriage as something he was happy about. On the contrary, from the earliest days of English settlement in Virginia, the official English policy had been to encourage such intermarriages because it was thought that they would promote peaceful interactions with the native population. Other than John Rolfe though, very few colonists were inclined to pursue such marriages and the Native Americans gave little indication of interest on their part. Given that situation, I feel confident in saying that the chances that my ancestor, Unity Harris, was a Native American are virtually nonexistent, her unusual name notwithstanding. Even though "Unity" is an unusual given name, it is nonetheless an English word so it seems odd that it would evoke Native Americans anyway.

---

[7] Gary B. Nash, *Red, White, and Black: The Peoples of Early North America* (Englewood Cliffs, NJ: Prentice-Hall, Inc., 1992), p. 282.

Fighters, Not Lovers

Unity Harris's first name is not the only possible source of the tradition of Native American ancestry among her descendants, however. As noted above, her husband Edward was related to Thomas Harris, who arrived in Virginia no later than 1616 and was still living in Henrico County in 1657. Thomas had a son, William Harris (born ca. 1629) who was killed in a battle with Native Americans near present-day Richmond, Virginia in 1679. This William *did* have a son named Edward but it is not clear at this point if William's Edward is the same Edward Harris whose wife was named Unity – in fact, it seems most likely that he was not. DNA testing has shown, however, that Unity Harris's husband Edward was related to William Harris somehow. The story of William Harris's death at the hands of Indians could easily have spawned the tradition of Native American ancestry among the descendants of his relative, Edward Harris.

This is far from the only case of interaction with Native Americans that may have spawned an oral tradition of Indian ancestry. Similar interactions may have played a role in the genesis of the story of Cherokee forbearers in the family of newly-elected Senator Elizabeth Warren of Massachusetts, who is a native of Oklahoma. Her alleged Cherokee ancestor was one of her great-great-great-grandmothers, born about 1794 in North Carolina. Some contradictory information exists in documents concerning her given name, but there is no question that her maiden name was Smith and that her husband was Jonathan Crawford, who died in 1841 in Tennessee, leaving her a widow with several children still at home. In the 1860 census of Bledsoe County, Tennessee, she is listed as Neoma Crawford. However, a late-in-life marriage record of one of her sons, William J. Crawford (recorded in Oklahoma) her maiden name is given as O.C. Smith (the "O" could have been for Oma, a possible nickname for Neoma).

Several professional genealogists, including the noted Cherokee researcher Twyla Barnes, have researched this family extensively and have found no evidence that Neoma (or O.C.) Smith Crawford was a Cherokee or from any tribe at all. She *was* born in North Carolina, one of the states the Cherokees resided in, but the members of this tribe were concentrated in the western North Carolina mountains, eastern Tennessee, and northern Georgia. Neoma Smith Crawford was born in Chatham County, in the Piedmont region of North Carolina, more than 200 miles east of any areas occupied by Cherokees and an unlikely residence for any Native Americans at all by the 1790s. Neoma's father, Wyatt Smith, along with siblings Isham, Jordan, Zadock, Wiley, Merrel, Elizabeth, and Holly, jointly sold a tract of land in Chatham County in 1805. The fact that these siblings were joint owners of this tract suggests that they inherited it from someone, most likely their parents, whose names remain unknown. This set of given names, however, hardly sounds like a large family of Native Americans who had somehow established themselves as landowners in a post-frontier area of white settlement in central North Carolina. Instead, these people appear to be from a family of European descent, more likely English than any other nationality. Some Smith families descend from Germans named Schmidt, but the given names in this family hint at British origins. The direct male-line ancestors of Wyatt Smith, as shown by DNA testing, were of the most common haplogroup found in Western European populations, thereby proving that at least that portion of their ancestry was European. Wyatt Smith was still living at the time of the 1850 census, aged 82 and while the maiden name of his wife remains uncertain (her given name was Margaret) she and Wyatt were both identified as white on the census records they appeared on from 1830 through 1850. The same is true of Jonathan Crawford and his wife, identified as white in the census records of 1830 and 1840. The widowed Neoma Crawford has not been found on the 1850 census but she is listed as white on the 1860 census. Testimony by Wyatt Smith on behalf of a Revolutionary War veteran named John Curtis, who applied for a pension, shows that the former resided in Chatham County as a teenager. There was no shortage of young white women there and the chances that there were more than a handful of Native American women there, even if he had been inclined to marry one, are virtually nil. Any such women who *might* have been there would not have been Cherokees.

So now one must consider the question of how the tradition of the Native American origins of Neoma (Smith) Crawford began. The circumstances of her father's life are one possible source. Wyatt Smith and some of his siblings relocated to Sumner County, Tennessee soon after the land sale of 1805 and for a brief period, in December 1813, he served in Colonel Robert Dyer's Regiment of the Tennessee Volunteer Cavalry and Mounted Gunmen – a regiment formed primarily to contain the Creek Indians, who had sided with the British in the War of 1812. Here is another instance of interaction with Native Americans – even though it involved fighting them – possibly spawning a tradition of a genetic tie to them.

There *Was* a Connection to the Trail of Tears

Another fact of Neoma (Smith) Crawford's life that could have sparked the oral history about her Cherokee origins involves her husband, Jonathan Crawford. Paul C. Reed, a Fellow of the American Society of Genealogists, apparently uncovered documentation showing that from late 1835 to late 1836, Jonathan served in the East Tennessee Mounted Infantry Volunteer Militia commanded by Brigadier General R. G. Dunlap. This unit participated in the rounding up of Cherokees for the purpose of removing them to Oklahoma along the route that later became known as the "Trail of Tears." The unit re-formed in late 1837 and went to Florida to participate in the Second Seminole War. Jonathan Crawford was, according to Reed's research, also a member of the unit during this time period.

Reed's research has been reported on by Michael Patrick Leahy, a political writer who is also an amateur genealogist himself. Leahy is also a staunch Republican who opposes Warren (a Democrat) politically, so his writings must be eyed with a certain element of suspicion. It is highly unlikely, however, that a professional genealogist the caliber of Paul Reed would risk his professional reputation by falsifying research in a public venue, knowing very well that another capable researcher could easily discredit his work if he did so. It is, perhaps, one of the great ironies of all oral history used by genealogists that a tradition of Native American ancestry can result from military action against native populations on the part of ancestors. Jonathan Crawford served in a military unit that took hostile actions against Native Americans. Ironically, his wife, Neoma (Smith) Crawford, became the focus of some of her descendants' assumptions of Indian ancestry – and for her, her husband's military service may have helped spawn the tradition.

Political Overtones – And Not Just for Politicians

The case of Elizabeth Warren's alleged Native American heritage may set a precedent in terms of motivating researchers to investigate such traditions more thoroughly – whether it is their own lineage or that of others. It is a cherished tradition in numerous American families of primarily European descent – and unlike most other oral history, it also has political overtones in the minds of many. The Warren case may be the first that has actually become a campaign issue – but for many whose families have the tradition it has taken on personal significance, regardless of their political views. White Americans of a liberal political persuasion often feel a significant amount of guilt over the mistreatment of racial minorities throughout the history of the United States. If they learn of family traditions of Native American ancestry, it can reduce the guilt somewhat – after all, it gives them a reason to believe they had ancestors who were oppressed too. People of a more conservative mindset can also develop an emotional stake in the idea that they are descendants of Native Americans. Some of them may use it as a shield against accusations of racism. These political motivations do not usually, in and of themselves, start traditions of native ancestry. However, when the traditions are already there, these motives may create an added personal investment in them and increase the chances that they will be passed on to future generations, regardless of their accuracy (or lack thereof) or the shakiness of the reasons the traditions actually began in the first place.

She Looks Like an Indian!

Another common source of oral history of a Native American ancestor is the simple physical appearance of people. I recall many casual researchers I have met over the years who have shown me 19th century photographs of elderly women with their hair tied back behind their heads. The claim "Look at her, she looks just like an Indian!" routinely follows on the heels of that. Very often, people who are just starting to take an interest in genealogy will jump to such conclusions upon seeing old photos of family members for the first time – not realizing how common it was for older American women to tie their hair in buns behind their heads in the 19th century. Before I ever saw a photo of my great-great-grandmother, Catherine Ann (Thrawls) Hite (1832-1917), I was told by one of my grandfather's cousins (who retained some memories of her, her death having occurred when he was seven) that *she* looked like an Indian. He did not have a photo at hand to show me but soon after, I located a nephew of his who did have one. The photo, taken in the early twentieth century when she was in her seventies, revealed just what I would have expected – an elderly woman with her hair tied back in a bun, but who had no other features that I would have remotely considered indicative of Native American heritage. This is the same great-great-grandmother who, on her death certificate, was falsely identified by her son as the daughter of a German immigrant. My grandmother

84

had told me that Catherine was Dutch and had never really learned to converse in English. It amazes me that I ever learned anything accurate about her when I consider how much contradictory information as I was given on her background – all of it false. Her actual background (what I know of it) is a mixture of English and Swiss as has been mentioned previously.

But Her Parents were German Immigrants

This is not the most obvious case of someone of European origins being mistaken for Native American based on a photo. At least one descendant of Helena (Schwerdt) Hite (1862-1947) said that *she* looked like an Indian in her picture. Helena married Christopher Sylvester Hite (1858-1929), a great-grandson of the original Christopher Hite and his wife Margaret, and they lived in Newry, Pennsylvania. Again, this was a marriage that took place long after any significant native populations lived in that region of Pennsylvania, but the idea that Helena could have been a Native American never made any sense anyway – her parents, Charles Schwerdt and Catherine Kolbenschlag, were both born in Germany! The descendant who made that comment about Helena's appearance may have known she was a child of German immigrants, but she could have inadvertently started an oral tradition of Native American ancestry had one of her children or grandchildren (who did not know of the German connection) heard her say this and repeated it to later generations. For all I know, she did.

Elusive Maiden Name? She Must Have Been an Indian!

All of the aforementioned examples (except that of Unity Harris) involve women whose alleged Native American origins have been disproven by documentary evidence. In the case of Unity Harris, two reasons have been suggested for the story of her supposed Indian background – the rarity of her given name and the death of her husband's relative at the hands of Native Americans. There is, however, a third possibility. Unity's maiden name, to this point, has not been determined and it is not at all unusual for researchers who grow frustrated at the lack of success in determining the family of origin of a female ancestor to simply throw up their hands and say "Oh, she must have been an Indian!" An added factor in such conclusions is that many Americans have a tradition of Native American ancestry somewhere in their lineage, but no knowledge of which branch of their ancestors it comes from. A female ancestor with an elusive maiden name often strikes these people as a likely candidate for that. However, a a more likely scenario in such cases is that the woman was from a family of modest means that left limited records.

My own ancestry abounds with women whose given names I have been able to find, but whose maiden names have so far eluded me. Unity Harris is just one example and she is one I have learned about only recently. She is not the only one, however, who brings a tradition of Native American heritage into my research. Another female ancestor I have recently learned of is Lydia (maiden name unknown, died 1828), the wife of Abraham Sovain (ca. 1741-1805). Abraham arrived in Philadelphia from Switzerland on the ship *Crawford* 26 October 1768. Some of Abraham and Lydia's descendants claim

Figure 4 - Catherine Ann (Thrawls) Hite (1832-1917), at left, with her daughter Emma Bell (Hite) Makadanz (1877-1967). The wife of one of Catherine's grandsons recalled that Catherine spoke only broken English and her death certificate (information provided by her son Simon Wesley Hite) identified her father as John Thrawls, a native of Germany. One of Emma's sons recalled that Catherine was at least partly (perhaps half) Native American, through her mother. Census records, however, proved that her father was Samuel Thrawls, who was born in Pennsylvania or Maryland, and this was augmented by the fact that she was named in Samuel's will. Her mother, as primary sources proved, was of mixed English, Swiss, and German ancestry – not a Native American. Poor Catherine – many of her grandchildren knew her well, but nothing anyone "remembered" about her background proved to be correct.

she was a Native American. Abraham's migration pattern in America, however, makes it unlikely that he would have ever encountered Native Americans prior to his marriage. For starters, he may have already been married before he left Europe, though that is not certain. Secondly, he apparently remained in the city of Philadelphia for at least two years after his arrival and it is almost certain that he was married before he left that city. It is hard to imagine anyone encountering Native Americans in Philadelphia as late as 1770. Third, his next residence was the growing town of Winchester, Virginia, which he served as its jailer during the Revolutionary War era. Indeed, Abraham Sovain seems to have spent nearly his entire life in America in cities or towns, living out his last few years in Sweet Springs in Monroe County in modern-day West Virginia (where he also served as jailer). The chances of him coming into contact with Native Americans at all, much less marrying one, seem virtually nil. The idea that his wife Lydia was a Native American probably results from the fact that her maiden name remains elusive. It may be that some of her descendants have heard a tradition of Native American lineage from an unspecified ancestor and see Lydia as a likely candidate simply because her maiden name has not been determined.

In the past two decades, I have exchanged e-mails and letters with numerous descendants of my Hite ancestors, Christopher and Margaret Hite, of Bedford County, Pennsylvania. A suggestion that I have begun receiving only in the past five years is that Margaret was a Native American. I have no doubt that this is a simple reaction to the fact that her maiden name has not yet been determined. Given that Christopher Hite was from one of the poorest families in the town of Bedford, it is only logical to believe that his wife came from a family of equally limited means. That fact alone could account for difficulty in identifying her family of origin. It is also possible that her father, whoever he was, died before her marriage to Christopher. That would account for the lack of a reference to a woman named Margaret Hite in any will or estate document in Bedford County. Christopher Hite, who lived through the terror of Pontiac's Rebellion as a young child in Bedford and who fought the Iroquois during the 1779 campaign against them led by General John Sullivan, seems as unlikely a candidate as anyone of his era to have married a Native American woman. The fact that he fought Native Americans could account for a tradition of Indian ancestry among his descendants but since the idea seems to have surfaced so recently, it is much more likely to stem primarily from the lack of documentation of his wife's maiden name. Again, some descendants may also have a tradition of Native American ancestry without any knowledge of where that alleged lineage stems from. Christopher and Margaret Hite and "Indian Eve" Earnest (mentioned in a previous chapter) have many mutual descendants. Even though Indian Eve was not actually a Native American (she simply lived with them as a captive for nine years) some of her descendants have misunderstood her life story and assumed she was an Indian.

Mixed Race Children – in *Native* Society

I am sure that by now, readers think I am convinced that all stories of marriages and liaisons between colonists and Native Americans are inaccurate. That is not the case – I know some are valid. I already mentioned Pocahontas, who married the English settler John Rolfe, lived in white society, and undoubtedly has tens of thousands of descendants living today – most of them of primarily European descent who, nonetheless, have a legitimate claim to Native American ancestry. I felt it was necessary to provide a wide variety of examples of false ones to illustrate how widespread the tradition is and how varied the situations are that can spawn such traditions. I also felt it necessary to show how easy it is to fall into the trap of taking these traditions for granted without researching them. It is, I think, important to point out the uniqueness of the case of John Rolfe and Pocahontas. Their marriage is the only one known between an English settler and a Native American in the early years of English settlement in Virginia that produced descendants who lived in English colonial society. There were, however, areas of the colonies that saw a more frequent occurrence of marriages and liaisons between European settlers and Native Americans. The historian Gary Nash, in his aforementioned work, notes that in such interaction was more frequent in the Carolinas and Georgia in the colonial era than in the other colonies. He cited examples in Georgia of John McDonald and Alexander Cameron, Deputy Indian Commissioners to the Cherokees, who took Native American wives a few years before the American Revolution.[8] It is, however, necessary to note that when these marriages did happen, the resulting offspring *were* far more likely to remain in native society than to be integrated into white society. McDonald is a case in point. His children grew up in Cherokee society and one of his grandchildren was John Ross, who served as the principal chief of the Cherokee nation from 1828 until 1860.

A recent monograph by historian Michelle LeMaster, *Brothers of One Mother: British-Native American Relations in the Colonial Southeast* includes an entire chapter on intermarriage between colonists and Native Americans. Her focus is not genealogy, of course, but genealogists can learn much from her work. Even though she uses the term "British" for people of European background, she is referring not only to people born in Great Britain, but all white residents of the British colonies in the modern-day southeastern United States, regardless of how long their families had been in the colonies or their ethnic origin. She describes at length the lives of traders of European origin who lived for extended periods among native societies in the backcountry of the Carolinas and Georgia. These traders acted as liaisons between colonial society further east and the numerous native cultures in the backcountry.

After the mid-eighteenth century, growing numbers of these traders married women from the societies they interacted with. The children of these marriages often grew up bilingual and many of *them* eventually assumed the role of emissary between the two societies. But, LeMaster notes, "The majority of mixed blood children in the southern interior lived most of their lives in native society and considered themselves Indian."[9] This is largely due to the fact that the tribes of that region saw the responsibility for educating and disciplining children as belonging to the mother's family. The British traders who married into these cultures often had no choice but to accept that arrangement even if they preferred not to – it had been a condition of the marriage in the first place. For boys in these societies, even those with Native American fathers,

---

[88] Nash, p. 283.
[9] Michelle LeMaster, *Brothers of One Mother: British-Native American Relations in the Colonial Southeast* (Charlottesville and London: University of Virginia Press, 2012), p. 173-174.

maternal uncles often played a larger role in their upbringing than their fathers did. The same was true of the Iroquois further north. Some of these boys grew up to fight on the side of their Native American relatives when war erupted between them and the whites. One of the most famous of these was Alexander McGillivray, who was born into the Wind Clan of the Creek tribe about 1750. Genetically he was three-quarters European, as his father was a Scottish-born trader named Lachlan McGillivray and his maternal grandfather was a French officer stationed at Fort Toulouse in modern-day Alabama. McGillivray, though, lived primarily among the Creeks and helped broker an alliance between the British and the Creeks during the Revolutionary War, becoming a colonel in the British Army although his military experience was limited. He later became the principal chief of the area known as the "Upper Creek towns." McGillivray's influence was not that unusual – being biracial, if one also had a certain amount of familiarity with both cultures, was often advantageous within native society. In these societies, race did not matter if one was seen as a member of the tribe – and if one's mother was a member, the race of the father was irrelevant. White society was never nearly as accepting of the people referred to as "half-breeds."

Rejected by White Society

Partly for this reason, it was rare for European traders to bring their biracial children back to white society and raise them there. White society simply did not accept these children and even if they had, the native societies they were born into were not eager to let them go. For that reason, there are far more descendants of these marriages today who have lived their lives identifying as Native American than as Caucasian. Many of them reside in states west of the Mississippi such as Oklahoma today and, though they identify as native, large numbers of them have European ancestors. There are many more of those people in the United States today than there are people of primarily European descent with distant Native American forbearers.

Nonetheless, these relationships offer insight into another source of oral history of Native American ancestry in white families. There were traders and other European men who spent significant time on the frontier that actually had two or more wives – one European and one or more who were Native Americans. An example of this was General Joseph Martin of Henry County, Virginia, who gave his name to Martinsville, the county seat of Henry County. After 1777, Martin served as the agent to the Cherokees for North Carolina and Virginia. He already had a white wife and some children but while in Cherokee territory, he took a Cherokee wife, who used the English name Betsy but was a daughter of Nan-ye-hi, a leader of the Cherokee Women's Council. Martin had two children by Betsy, but they remained in Cherokee society[10]- even though they, like many other biracial children in native communities used their European father's surname. It would not be at all surprising though, if the story of Martin's marriage to the daughter of Nan-ye-hi sparked a tradition among at least some of his descendants by his European wife that they were of Native American heritage. Martin is far from the only man in colonial America who married into native society even while maintaining a Caucasian

---

[10] Cynthia Cumfer, *Separate Peoples, One Land: The Minds of Cherokees, Whites, and Blacks on the Tennessee Frontier* (Chapel Hill: University of North Carolina Press, 2007), p. 35.

family further east – and others who did were not necessarily as prominent as he was. Some of these families undoubtedly have traditions of Native American ancestry that are not accurate – another example of interactions with Native Americans that led to oral histories of lineage to them. Such marriages could have even found their way into primary sources in some cases – probably not a public record, but possibly into a journal kept by a trader or one of his friends. A reference in a journal such as "John Doe married the chief's daughter today" would not prove that the "chief's daughter" was the mother of John Doe's children who lived in European society. It is possible that John Doe also have had a white wife in colonial society whom he had already had children by – and may have returned to and had more children with after a sojourn among Native Americans. But such a reference could easily have spawned an oral tradition among John Doe's descendants by his Caucasian wife that they had a Native American ancestor.

Perhaps it was an Aunt by Marriage

Such "additional marriages" (marriages into native societies by traders and other white men who already had white wives) could be the source of numerous claims of native lineage – not only among their own descendants, but also among descendants of these traders' siblings and other close relatives. As an example, if the aforementioned John McDonald, grandfather of the Cherokee chief John Ross, had any siblings in the colonies, they probably knew of his marriage to a Cherokee woman. If they told the story to later generations who later passed it further down, it could easily have been distorted into a story among McDonald's distant nieces and nephews that this woman was a direct ancestor, rather than the wife of an uncle many generations back. This sort of tradition reflects the same principle, discussed in an earlier chapter, of how inaccurate maiden names for women can be introduced into one's lineage. In a previous chapter on this subject, I noted that my grandmother's mistaken idea that the maiden name of her great-grandmother Bagley was Tewksbury stemmed from the fact that a man with the Tewksbury surname had married a female Bagley relative. This marriage does mean that we had relatives with the Tewksbury surname, but we are not Tewksbury descendants. By the same token, the descendants of the siblings of John McDonald (and others who married into native societies) have Indian relatives who remained in native society. In McDonald's case, descendants of his siblings can accurately claim that they are related to the Cherokee chief John Ross. They do not, however, have Native American ancestry – John Ross had European ancestry and that is the lineage the descendants of his maternal grandfather McDonald's siblings have in common with him.

None of the preceding examples of biracial children remaining in native society are implied to mean that *none* of them ever lived in, and established families, in white communities. Professional historians have noted that some of these children who *did* remain in native society were genetically more European than native – John Ross, for example, was seven-eighths European. It would be naïve to assume that *none* of these children, particularly those who were mostly European and could pass for white, slipped covertly into white society and raised families there. No ethnic group is monolithic in its thinking. Even if most preferred to remain in native society – or had no choice in the matter – some of the "whiter" ones might have found white American culture more appealing and found a way to disappear into it. It is certain that some biracial children who were of mixed European and African background succeeded in that effort. They had far greater motivation of course – an escape from slavery or, if already free, an escape from the threat of being enslaved. One example of this involves two of Thomas Jefferson's children by his slave Sally Hemings. Beverly and Harriet Hemings were no more than one-eighth African in their genetic makeup but because their mother was a slave, they were slaves. Nonetheless, their physical appearance enabled them to conceal their African heritage and escape into white society. Both married Caucasians (apparently unidentified) who may or may not have known of their African lineage.[11] Because of the lack of information on descendants of these two former slaves, there is no way of knowing at this point what oral traditions about the origins of Beverly and Harriet Hemings may have been passed down in their families.

Were They Actually African-American?

It is worthwhile to note that because people of African descent have more motivation to assimilate into white society than Native Americans did, one must consider the possibility that some primarily European families with a tradition of Native American ancestry may actually have African ancestry instead. For white people in America, until the last quarter or so of the twentieth century, there was far more of a stigma attached to African lineage than to Native American background. This was especially true in the southern states, where all three groups had the most extensive history of interaction. For that reason, people of primarily European background, whose physical appearance was not "white enough", may have attempted to explain it away by claiming a Native American ancestor. The original claimants may have known that the claim was untrue but their children and grandchildren who heard it may have assumed it was valid.

The depth of the stigma attached to African ancestry is illustrated in a reference by historian Melton McLaurin in his 1987 work *Separate Pasts: Growing up White in the Segregated South*. McLaurin wrote of his own upbringing in the small town of Wade, North Carolina, which is only three miles from my own childhood home. An episode he described was his interest in dating a girl in Wade (who had blond hair and blue eyes) during his adolescence (in the 1950's), which was discouraged by his mother and grandmother. When he pressed for details, his grandmother informed him of the girl's great-great-grandmother who was, according to her account, a "high yellow". That is a term I remember very well from my own childhood. It refers to someone who is, at most, one-quarter African, but otherwise Caucasian. Still, in the community of my childhood, such a person was generally regarded as African-American. In the case of the girl McLaurin had expressed an attraction to, her African background apparently amounted to no more than one sixty-fourth of her lineage. For McLaurin's grandmother, however, that was enough to raise the specter of the possibility of great-grandchildren with "kinky hair and flat noses" while informing her grandson that the children of the girl's aunt, who

---

[11] Annette Gordon-Reed, *The Hemingses of Monticello: An American Family* (New York, London: W.W. Norton & Company), p. 601.

91

lived in a neighboring town, did possess such traits[12] She had also noted that the girl's father had left her mother when he learned of the African ancestry. This was a girl who, from her description, seems to have easily passed as entirely Caucasian. If white Southerners of her adolescence considered her limited African heritage a barrier, it is easy to imagine what those who were actually more dark complexioned must have faced. There was no indication that this young girl's family claimed Native American heritage but it is easy to imagine such a story being made up as a substitute for actual African ancestry in those circumstances – and in some cases, those traditions may have been passed along even when the stigma of African heritage had lessened.

A discussion of Native American tradition as an alternative to African realities brings to mind the group known as *Melungeons* – mostly dark complexioned people, often with Caucasian features, that established themselves long ago in the southern Appalachian regions. The legends about this group are many – but one of the most prominent is that they are partly Native American, more specifically Cherokee (here we go again). Another legend is that they descend from Portuguese or Middle Easterners who somehow made it to the modern-day United States even before the earliest English settlements in the Chesapeake regions of the early 17th century. Recent DNA testing, however, suggests that these people are primarily, if not entirely, simply a mix of European and African. More specifically, the mitochondrial DNA of the test subject descendants – passed through female lines – indicates European origins. The Y-chromosome passed through male lines, shows European origins in some cases and African origins in others. To professional historians, the conclusion of this DNA testing is perfectly logical. The Melungeons are the descendants of children produced by African men and European women in eastern Virginia. Because children inherited the condition (slave or free) of their mothers during the era of slavery, regardless of the status of their fathers, the ancestors of these people would not have been slaves. Nonetheless, they would have faced significant discrimination and so they had definite motivation for moving into a more isolated area further west. Undoubtedly, there are descendants of these Melungeons today that appear primarily white, but who have a tradition of Native American ancestry that is actually African. Like the descendants of European traders and native women, these people are found primarily in the South. It should be noted that the test the subjects of this study took was not the Family Finder test – the one that gives a complete racial breakdown of an individual. Instead, it only identified the Y-chromosome and mitochondrial DNA – direct male and direct female lineage, respectively. However one would assume that if other racial groups comprised a significant segment of the ancestry of the Melungeons, they would have turned up in at least a few of the test subjects.

Gary Nash's work identifies the Carolinas and Georgia as being the areas of European settlement that saw the most sexual intermingling between Europeans and Native Americans – at least in what is now the United States. He notes that interracial marriages were almost unheard of in New England and the Middle Colonies, where Europeans came as families from the very beginning rather than as single men. The

---

[12] Melton A. McLaurin, *Separate Pasts: Growing Up White in the Segregated South* (Athens: University of Georgia Press), p. 73-75.

possibility of such marriages was further diminished in these areas – particularly in New England - by the rapid decimation of the native populations due to epidemics. Nash does not mention the Germans who settled along the Hudson River in New York in 1710, many of whom relocated to the Schoharie region west of Albany by the middle of the decade. A 2004 book by historian Philip Otterness *Becoming German: The 1709 Palatine Migration to New York* does illuminate the experiences of this group. The Germans who moved to the Schoharie Valley immediately established interpersonal relationships with the neighboring Mohawks, in some cases allowing their children to be "adopted" into the tribe, though it is not clear how frequently this relationship led to intermarriage. As with the southern colonies, most of the marriages that did occur probably resulted in children who remained with the Mohawks rather than living in white society. In a presentation I attended in the summer of 2012, Otterness noted that the Mohawks, for their part, note the existence of a few German surnames among the modern-day members of their tribe. *Dochstader* (spelling varies) is perhaps the most widespread.

A More Common Canadian Phenomenon

For modern-day residents of the northeast, the most likely source of Native American ancestry comes through connections to Canada. In the late 19th and early 20th centuries, many Canadians – particularly French Canadians - came to New England for jobs in mills. From the very earliest days of French settlement in Canada, French men tended to come alone and many had no hesitation about taking Native American wives. British in Canada, possibly influenced by the French there, were also more likely than those in the United States to marry native women and raise families with them, whether in Native American or white society. Among the very few cases I am personally acquainted with of an accurate tradition of Native American ancestry involves some close friends of mine in Rhode Island, where I now live. I was eating lunch with one of them a few years ago when she mentioned a great-grandmother who had been three-quarters Native American. Usually, my initial reaction would be one of skepticism, having heard so many stories of Native American lineage in my thirty years of genealogical research. This, however, was a pretty recent connection and I knew that this woman's grandparents were all still living. Later, I gave it even more thought. The place this great-grandmother had lived – Laconia, New Hampshire – was not at all far from the Canadian border. I did not have a name, so I did a search of the 1930 census of Laconia for anyone that might be designated as "Indian" in the race column. One family came up in the search – a family with the surname McEwan, all of whom had been born in Canada. The next time I spoke to this friend, I asked her the name of this Native American great-grandmother, hoping she would know. She was very specific – Olive McEwan. Olive's husband's name had been William Cole.

From there, the Native American ancestry was easy to prove. The 1930 census listed William and Olive Cole as aged 38 and 31 respectively with six children, ages 1 to 10. Olive's birthplace was given more specifically as Nova Scotia. From there, a check of immigration records noted her arrival in Houlton, Maine in 1918, aged 20. The record referred to her as an Indian, born in Bear River, Nova Scotia, daughter of John McEwan.

Her complexion was described as dark, her hair black, but her eyes were noted as blue, which suggested she was not entirely Native American. Further research in Canadian records demonstrated that she was, in fact, three quarters Native American. Her paternal grandfather, Michael McEwan, had been from Scotland, but Michael's wife, Victoria Siah, was of the Micmac (or Mi'kmaq) tribe. Olive's mother, Mary Charlotte Pictou, was also a Mi'kmaq and Olive had grown up on the Bear River Reserve in Digby County, Nova Scotia. So the Native American ancestry of my friends was verified. From there, it was possible to trace some of the lineage further. Mary Charlotte Pictou, born about 1875 according to the 1881 census, was a daughter of Noel Pictou (born ca. 1843 in Bear River) and Francoise Barthelmy (born ca. 1846 in nearby Salmon River), both identified as Indians on their marriage record of 8 October 1866 in Digby County. This record gave *their* parents' names also – Benjamin and Mary Pictou for Noel and Etienne and Marie Barthelmy for Francoise – all again identified as Indians. Olive's paternal grandparents, Michael and Victoria (Siah) McEwan have not been found on census records but one of their grandsons, in writing, made reference to a brother of Victoria's named Solomon Siah.[13] Solomon does appear on the census in Bear River, aged 60 in 1881 and he is also listed as an Indian. So for Olive McEwan Cole (1898-1873) there is no indication in public records that she had any known European ancestors other than through her paternal grandfather, Michael McEwan.

Olive McEwan was the first, but not the only member of this family to migrate to the United States. The Native American McEwan household enumerated in the 1930 census of Laconia was headed by Olive's stepmother, Minnie McEwan (Mary Charlotte had apparently died in 1904 or a little later), and included Olive's younger half-siblings. All had arrived in the United States in the late 1920s. Interestingly, one of these half-siblings, J. Richard McEwan (born in 1908) eventually returned to Nova Scotia, settled on the reserve once again, and lived out his life there, serving as chief from 1963-1975. His son Gregory was elected to the post in 1979. This reserve still exists as Bear River First Nation and my friends still have relatives there. Richard published an account of his experiences in 1988 titled *Memories of a Micmac Life*. At least one other half-sibling of Olive, however (a sister named Phyllis, born in 1918) lived in Massachusetts and married a man named Leroy Schultz, by whom she had four children.[14] So there are other McEwan descendants of verifiable Native American ancestry in New England besides the descendants of Olive McEwan Cole. Obviously, these McEwans were not the only Canadians with native ancestors who came to New England in the later 19th or early 20th centuries. Anyone with such an ancestor who has a tradition of native background should try to locate the person on immigration records or Canadian census records. If the ancestor was, in fact, a Native American, these documents should say so.

In thirty years of genealogical research, I have met many people who claimed Native American ancestry. Traditions of it have turned up in no fewer than six of my own ancestral families, some of which were mentioned earlier in this chapter. For four of the lineages, I am confident that I have disproven it. The other two have not been

---

[13] J. Richard McEwan, *Memories of a Micmac Life* (Fredericton, New Brunswick: Micmac Maliseet Institute, University of New Brunswick, 1988), pp. 2-4.
[14] McEwan, X-XI.

Figure 5 - This manifest of passengers applying for admission to the United States in Houlton, Maine in 1918, lists Olive McEwan, age 20, on Line 18 (7th from the bottom). Her entry under Column 10 (race or people) clearly identifies her as an Indian.

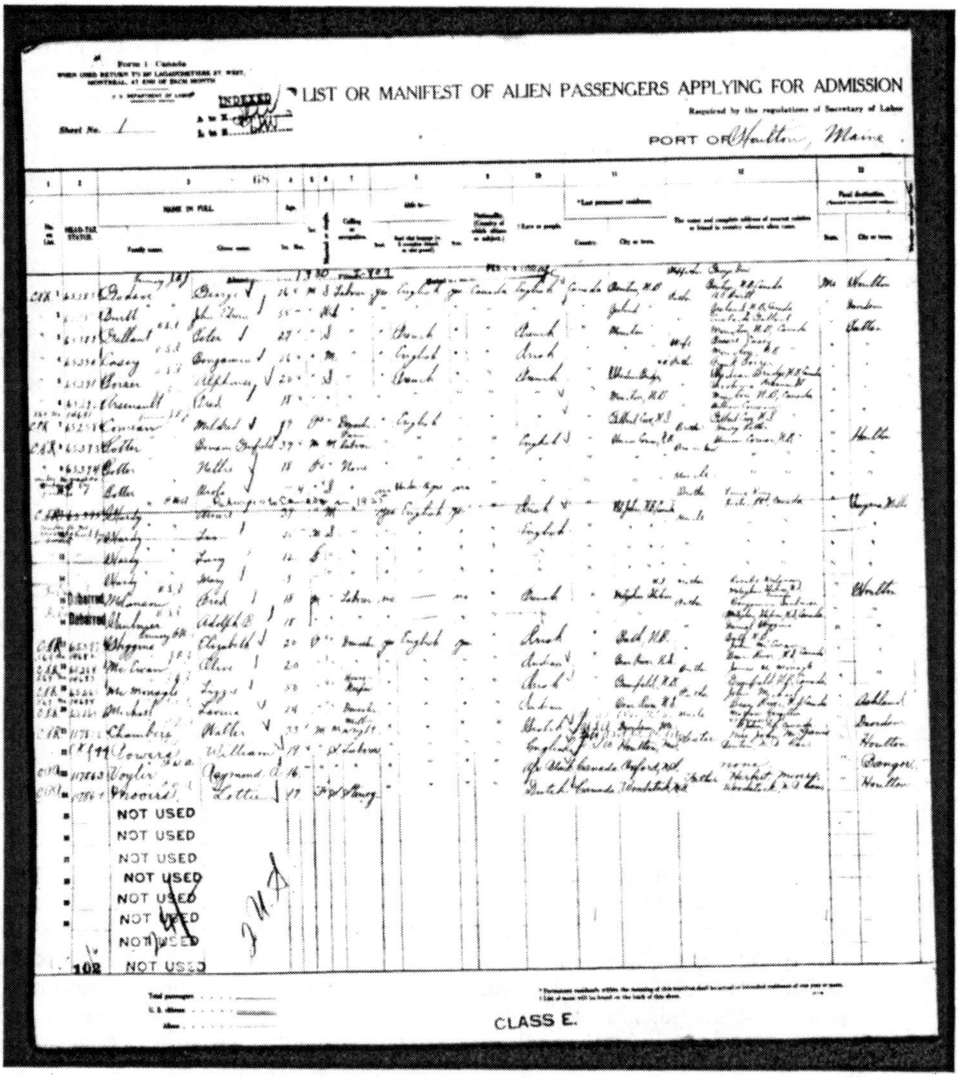
LIST OR MANIFEST OF ALIEN PASSENGERS APPLYING FOR ADMISSION

PORT OF Houlton, Maine

INDEXED

NOT USED

NOT USED

NOT USED

NOT USED

NOT USED

NOT USED

NOT USED

NOT USED

CLASS E.

disproven, but I have serious doubts in both cases. In other cases I have helped friends with their researches that have traditions of Native American heritage in their own families. The descendants of Olive (McEwan) Cole are the only ones I have confirmed it for – and they already knew. Some of their close relatives in New Hampshire had already visited the Bear River First Nation Reserve, the childhood home of Olive – but I did not know of that before I did the research. Thinking back, I remember that I had always assumed that my friend that told me the story was partly of Italian or Portuguese heritage – she has very dark hair and those two ethnic groups have a significant presence in Rhode Island. Native American had never occurred to me as a possibility.

How the Popular Media Bolstered the Legend

As I think back even more, I cannot help but believe that in addition to the possible sources of the Native American tradition already mentioned, popular culture must have played a role in fomenting them. I remember seeing reruns of TV shows of the western genre during the 1970s. Some of those shows often unrealistically depicted Native Americans living in white society and being accepted as part of the community. The character of Mingo on the *Daniel Boone* show (starring Fess Parker as Boone) comes to mind. Mingo was not based on any real person, but he was cast as a character with a European father and Native American mother who had somehow been educated at Oxford but had ultimately ended up on the Kentucky frontier. The character was a close friend of Boone and lived in or around Boonesborough. He was not depicted with a wife and children, but the possibility that he could marry a white woman did not seem farfetched. I also recall a single episode of the long running series *Bonanza* that cast Dawn Wells (later to gain fame as Mary Ann on *Gilligan's Island*) as a Native American who married a young Caucasian friend of the main characters on the show (the Cartwright family) and presumably went on to have a family in white society.

Only a few years after those shows were on the air, the pop star Cher popularized a song titled *Half-Breed* which concerned a fictitious woman whose mother had been a "pure Cherokee" (again – did any white man every marry into any other tribe?) and who had faced discrimination from both sides throughout her life. The song does not identify an era, but while discrimination from white society would have been likely in such a circumstance, a Cherokee mother would have ensured acceptance into this matriarchal culture regardless of the race of the father. This fact contradicts the sentiments of one of the lines in the song "The Indians said that I was white by law". Again, one wonders how much this song influenced people to believe in an exaggerated frequency of interracial marriage in the past. More recently, I obtained a humorous book based on the long running animated TV series *The Simpsons* titled *Matt Groenings's The Simpsons: Uncensored Family Album*. Among other things, the book constructs a family tree for these fictitious characters, complete with drawings. Among the ancestors depicted for the family – 4th-great-grandparents of patriarch Homer Simpson – are Rupert Simpson and his wife, Winifred Running Goat. The character of Winifred, drawn with braided hair and a headband around her head, is unquestionably a Native American. Her father, Joe Puffing Goat, has also braided hair with feathers and is smoking a pipe – presumably a peace pipe. Joe's wife, Mary Frowning Cloud, is shown with braided hair and a headband just like her fictitious daughter.

Insights from Historians

Such fictitious depictions of Native Americans living as fully accepted members of white society, whether in colonial times or in the 19th century American West, have undoubtedly made the traditions of native heritage more believable to those who have heard the stories from their grandparents or other older relatives. Far more useful, though, is the work of academic historians. Very few academics have much interest in genealogy of its own sake, but they often use it as a methodology for proving major points about historical topics. The work of historians like Gary Nash and Michelle LeMaster is invaluable for beginning genealogists who have traditions of Native American ancestors. These historians and others like them have a profound interest in the interactions of the various racial groups in colonial and 19th century America. Their work can inform genealogists of how likely (or unlikely) their tradition of Native American ancestry really is.

Some Want the Benefits

As with every other oral tradition, genealogists should never assume that the verbally transmitted history of Native American ancestry is accurate. There are far too many variables that can falsely spawn such traditions - unusual given names (particularly female names), interactions with Native Americans other than marriage (running the gamut from trading with them to warring with them), physical appearance, elusive maiden names, and collateral relatives who produced biracial children that remained in Indian society. This tradition is one that many people have a strong desire to believe – sometimes due to political leanings and at other times due to potential tangible benefits. I once received a call from another descendant of my great-great-grandmother Catherine Ann (Thrawls) Hite – one I had never met – who asked about the tradition of her being half Indian. When I told him it was unproven and I doubted it was true, he expressed disappointment – not due to any strong interest in his background, but because he was hoping to obtain minority status for financial aid for college. As a professional archivist, I also know of instances when archival institutions have been flooded with researchers trying to document family links to specific tribes - after the tribes obtained permits to open casinos. The goal is to obtain a share of the profits.

DNA *Can* Help – Up to a Point

Regardless of the motivation for researching oral traditions of Native American heritage, the search should be approached just like any other research – following the path wherever it leads. DNA testing is a possibility, but it is not foolproof. I recently took a DNA test called the Family Finder test. This test enables one to find relatives who have taken the same test regardless of how they are related, as long as there is a certain amount of DNA in common. However, it also shows what percentage of one's DNA comes from each of the major racial groups. My own test revealed that approximately

93.18 percent of my heritage is Western European – not at all a surprise. The remaining percentage – 6.82 – is Middle Eastern. This, I have no doubt, stems from interactions between Europe and the Middle East in medieval times or earlier (though I might have suspected I had Melungeon ancestors prior to the DNA evidence that cast doubt on their alleged Middle Eastern origins). I show no trace of Native American, African, Asian, or any other racial group. That does not entirely disprove that I have no ancestors of any of those groups. As an example, if one 5th great-grandparent was Native American or African, that ancestor would account for only 1/128 of my heritage – less than one percent. It would certainly be possible that I did not happen to inherit any DNA from that single ancestor. Had my test revealed African or Native American DNA, it would have proven I had someone of that background in my lineage. The fact that none of that DNA appeared in my test results does not absolutely prove that I have none of that ancestry – but in all my years of research I have never found a reliable clue that made me suspect the possibility of either.

Chances are, if a descendant of Olive (McEwan) Cole took the Family Finder test, the Native American lineage would show up. Her great-granddaughter who told me about her is 3/32 Native American – nearly ten percent. This friend's mother, who is also a friend of mine, is 3/16 Native American – almost twenty percent. Such a recent connection as that is almost guaranteed to manifest itself in a Family Finder test. But for someone who is no more than 1/128 Native American (or African), there is a very real possibility that the Family Finder test would not reveal it at all. That being the case, traditional research methods – going through documents – probably offers the best hope for an answer. The most important thing to remember is not to close one's mind to the possibility that the story is wrong.

When I think about Catherine Ann (Thrawls) Hite, my great-great-grandmother, I am grateful that I did not learn of the tradition of her Native American heritage until I had a few years of research experience under my belt. Although I learned her father's name very soon after identifying her, the identity of her mother (who died before the 1850 census) eluded me for several years. I could have easily fallen into the trap of assuming she was a Native American whose name I would never be able to turn up. Even after I did learn her name from her marriage record – Elizabeth Huff – and the dates of her life from her tombstone (1813-1844) I found research on her ancestry unexpectedly challenging for a number of years. I could have easily assumed – as some less-experienced genealogists may have – that she was a Native American who had adopted the name "Elizabeth Huff" upon being converted to Christianity. Her children were all born in Harrison County, Ohio, a county just east of the county of Tuscarawas, where Moravian missionaries had settled with a community of Christian Indians prior to the American Revolution. The "breakthrough document" that finally cracked the case of Elizabeth (Huff) Thrawls's ancestry was an 1847 deed of the sale of some land that her mother, Mary (Hiestand) Huff had patented in 1830. The fact that her mother rather than her father patented the land was part of why it had been so difficult to locate the documentation of the lineage. Mary, whose husband Thomas Huff was still alive at the time, had somehow patented the land in her own right – a surprising occurrence in that era. The sale of her land netted 900 dollars after her death and her husband, who survived her, received 400 dollars of it – slightly more than a traditional dower. Mary's four surviving children each received 100 dollars from the sale and Elizabeth's share (100 dollars) was placed in the trust of her husband, Samuel Thrawls, for their children, all of whom were still minors at the time.

An Early Feminist, Not a Native American

The circumstances of this land patent and its subsequent distribution cast Mary (Hiestand) Huff as an early feminist of sorts – an interesting ancestor that I might never have found had I accepted the Native American story about her granddaughter Catherine (Thrawls) Hite without question. Mary's exclusive ownership of land as a married woman reflects, in a sense, the matriarchal nature of numerous native tribes and raises the question about whether or not that could have given rise to the Native American tradition associated with Catherine. That is highly unlikely – it is far more probable that the tradition resulted solely from the impression some of her descendants had that she looked like an Indian – but such an idea is no less logical than someone who was her father's "little princess" being transformed by her descendants into a Cherokee princess.

In the final analysis, the best approach to traditions of Native American ancestry is the same as oral history of royal or noble lineage. Genealogists should not take the stories for granted and should follow whatever path their research leads them down. If the evidence for Native American ancestry is there, it will be found. Researchers must, however, tread carefully with such evidence. Even if one finds documentation of an ancestor of European descent marrying a Native American (such as in a trader's journal entry) the possibility – or more accurately, the likelihood – that this was an "additional" marriage for a man who already had a Caucasian wife must be examined. Discerning researchers should also watch carefully for other events in their ancestors' lives that could have led to a false story of native origins. For those of mostly European origin, the royal or noble ancestry is almost certainly there somewhere. The Native American traditions are far less likely to be true.

Chapter 11 - How Much Misinformation Can be Crammed Into One Paragraph?

If the following paragraph, taken directly from Otto A. Rothert's 1913 book *A History of Muhlenberg County* is any indication, the answer is "Quite a bit." The Muhlenberg County of the title of the book is in Kentucky.

Major Jesse Oates was born in North Carolina about the year 1756. He was a son of Jesse Oates Sr., who, although not a soldier in the Revolution did much toward promoting the war. Jesse Oates, Jr., however, much to the satisfaction of his father, took an active part in the struggle. After the Revolution Jesse Oates, Sr. gave his son Jesse practically all his estate, to the exclusion of his son-in-law Coghill, who it was said was either not in sympathy with the American colonies or was an outright Tory. Having received none of the expected fortune, Coghill's feeling toward his brother-in-law was anything but friendly.[15]

This brief paragraph, containing exactly 107 words, is a prime example of what I have referred to as written oral history. Major Jesse Oates, the subject of the paragraph, had died in 1831, eighty-two years before the book was written. His descendants were undoubtedly the source of the author's information. As will be shown, this short paragraph contains no fewer than five significant errors. Before analyzing those errors, however, it is necessary to quote the paragraph that followed this one in Rothert's work –

In those days, every man was obliged to attend the militia musters, which took place once a month. Coghill and Oates were members of the same company, and on nearly every drilling day a fight would take place between the two. Coghill was large and strong, Oates was small; the consequence was that Oates got the worst of the fight every time. Matters went on this way for several years, when one day Oates notified his brother-in-law that if he attacked him at the next muster he would kill him. The day arrived and Coghill, according to his custom, gave Oates his usual whipping. Oates had his flintlock with him and threatened to shoot, and would have done so had Coghill not begged him to give him a chance for his life. Oates agreed to let Coghill go home – a distance of two miles – to get the gun he preferred to use in this duel instead of the one he had with him. The two men and some of their friends mounted their horses and started for Coghill's farm. When the crowd arrived at the end of the short lane leading up to the house, Coghill put spurs to his horse and told Oates to shoot. Coghill evidently felt confident that Oates would miss him, and that his gun being loaded he could kill Oates before Oates could reload. Oates fired and killed Coghill instantly.[16]

This episode was what prompted Jesse Oates's move to Kentucky. It is impossible to know how accurate the details provided in the second paragraph are. However, the inaccuracies in the first paragraph are immediately apparent to anyone who has researched the genealogy of the families involved here in primary sources.

---

[15] Otto A. Rothert, *A History of Muhlenberg County* (Louisville, KY: John P. Morton & Company, 1913), p. 91.
[16] Rothert, pp. 91-92.

An Inaccuracy Every Twenty Words

First of all, "Major" Jesse Oates's father was not named Jesse Oates. Instead, his name was Jethro Oates (ca. 1732-1780). Secondly, there are serious doubts about the role Jethro Oates played in promoting the colonial cause in the Revolutionary War that require elaboration. Third, Jethro Oates's will, probated in Duplin County, North Carolina in January 1781, divided his estate equally among six of his eight children, including Jesse, after he settled some slaves and personal items on two older married daughters, neither of whose husband was the man Jesse Oates later killed. Fourth, the surname of the man Jesse Oates killed was *Cogdell*, not Coghill. Jesse's adversary was David Cogdell (1753-1802) and he was not Jesse's brother-in-law. Instead, Cogdell's daughter, Susannah, married Jesse Oates's youngest brother, John Oates (1775-1827). John, being only five years old when his father died, was still many years away from marriage and the terms of his father's will could hardly have mattered to David Cogdell at the time it was probated – and John got the same share of the estate as Jesse anyway. Finally, there is no evidence that David Cogdell was a Tory – in fact, just the opposite. Cogdell was a delegate, representing Wayne County, to the second North Carolina Constitutional Convention in the town of Fayetteville in 1789. While this was six years after the end of the war, it seems preposterous to believe that a former Loyalist would have been considered for such a duty.

It is worth noting at this point that I am a descendant of both of the families involved in this story. Jesse Oates's sister, Amia Oates (1761-1824), married Stephen King (1756-1812) of present-day Sampson County, North Carolina, a county formed from Duplin County in 1785. Two of their children John King (1789-1844) and Ann King (1795-1867) married, respectively, to Ann Cogdell (1793-1838) and Lewis Cogdell (1783-1861), children of David Cogdell. Both of these couples are direct ancestors of mine – therefore I am twice descended from David Cogdell, the loser of the conflict with Jesse Oates. Though I am not a direct descendant of Jesse, I am twice descended from his father, Jethro Oates, whose role in this scenario was as badly distorted as that of David Cogdell by the published Muhlenberg County history.

There *Was* a Tory – Just Not Him

David Cogdell, as noted, is hardly likely to have been a Loyalist during the American Revolution. I have found no evidence that he served in the Continental Army at any time, but the fact that he served as a delegate to the 1789 Constitutional Convention suggests that his sympathies had been with the Patriot cause during the war. While one cannot assume families were unified during this time period in the side they supported, it is perhaps noteworthy that David's much older brother, Richard Cogdell (1724-1787) was President of the New Bern Committee of Safety – a Continental organization - throughout the war. As for Jesse Oates, there are pay vouchers that indicate he served in militia units during the war and David Cogdell may have also served in such units. This was required of all able-bodied men of a certain age though and is not necessarily indicative of their sentiments during the war. There is, however, concrete evidence of the sympathies of Jesse's father, Jethro Oates.

On 15 June 1780, Jethro Oates was brought before court of Craven County, North Carolina, charged with "high treason" against the state. The charges were based on depositions by Simon Alderman and Silas Linton, both of whom were Continental Army soldiers who had escaped Charleston, South Carolina after the American surrender there, along with some others. Alderman and Linton told of encountering Jethro Oates on 8 June, three miles from South River in North Carolina, who had mistaken them for British soldiers and called them friends. Alderman further testified that Oates told them that General Caswell (Richard Caswell, a Patriot General) was "embodying men to go against them, the British" and that "the Rebels had wanted his (Oates's) corn, but that he had saved it for the British." Alderman further testified that Oates told him "he had information to give them of the strength of General Caswell, what arms and ammunition they had, that he offered to go with the deponent and the others (still thinking they were British) through the wood and reconnoitre (sp) the ground where the Americans were..." Jethro Oates signed an examination taken before the court which noted that had intended to avail himself of a protection from Patrick Stewart whom he had been informed was greatly in the interest of the British king. The examination further notes that Oates confessed to the soldiers "that he was a friend to the English, that he was secured by said soldiers and brought to New Bern." New Bern is the county seat of Craven County. There is no mistaking the handwriting on the signature affixed to the record of this examination. The signer is the same Jethro Oates who signed his will two months later.

There is no ambiguity here. Jethro Oates, the father of Jesse Oates, took actions supporting the British cause in 1780. By that point in the war, Jethro was unquestionably a Loyalist and it is actually surprising that the Continentals did not immediately hang him as a spy. What happened after that is not entirely clear. The case was committed to the Superior Court of the District of New Bern for 15 November 1780. However, the records of that session make no mention of Jethro Oates. Jethro signed his will on 30 August 1780, two and a half months before his scheduled trial. By January 1781, he was dead. There is no evidence that he was hanged for treason – although that is almost certainly the fate that awaited him if he had been tried. Perhaps he fell ill as a result of the conditions in the jail he was held in. His will does note that he was "weak in body" even though he was only forty-eight years old.

A Local Rivalry

Without question, this raises other possibilities about the source of the dispute between Jesse Oates and David Cogdell. By 1802, when the fatal conflict took place, John Oates (Jesse's brother) and Susannah Cogdell (David's daughter) had been married for a few years. Regardless of what Jesse's sympathies had been during the war, or his own feelings on the matter by the early 19th century, he probably would have found it difficult to allow any disparaging comments about his father's actions to go unchallenged. Both families were rather prominent in the area and while it seems odd that David and Jesse would have served in the same militia company since they lived in bordering counties (David in Wayne County, Jesse in Sampson County) they certainly moved in the same circles and had many mutual acquaintances. David may not have

Figure 6 - The document on top is the examination of Jethro Oates for treason in the court of Craven County, North Carolina, 15 June 1780. Below is the last page of his will, dated 30 August 1780. Oates's signatures on the two documents look very similar, though a tear in the will obscures part of the signature there. James Oates, who also signed the will, was a witness.

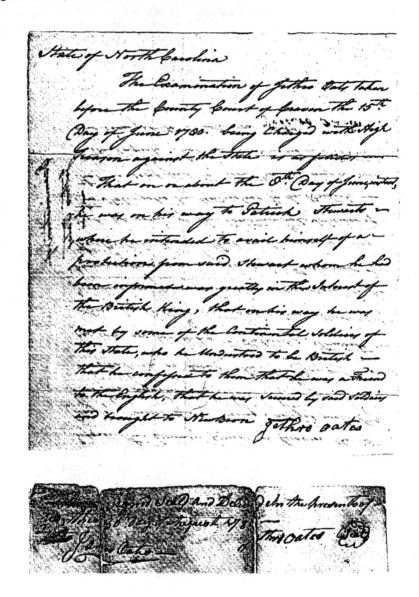

liked the fact that his daughter had married the son of a Tory and may have had no hesitation about saying so. David's brother Richard was a close friend of Richard Caswell, the General that Jethro Oates informed on. Whether David made remarks critical of Jethro directly to Jesse or if word of it simply got back to Jesse, this was a culture of masculine honor – and the honor of a deceased father must have been of paramount importance. All of this is speculation of course – perhaps Jesse Oates and David Cogdell simply disliked each other for reasons that had nothing to do with their families. Nonetheless, the tradition in the Oates family in Kentucky (Jesse's descendants), written by Otto Rothert in 1913 does imply that lingering animosities from the Revolutionary War may have played a role in the dispute. If that *was* a factor, it is clear that the Oates descendants flip-flopped the sympathies of their ancestors with those of the family's antagonist.

A Neighborhood Bully

There *is* documentary evidence that David Cogdell was a troublesome person who may have incited Jesse Oates to violence against him. In December 1803, five residents of Sampson County presented a petition to the Governor and General Assembly of North Carolina asking that Oates be pardoned for killing Cogdell. The petition described Cogdell as "*a person of the most turbulent and tumultuous conduct and manners a common disturber of the peace and by reason of his great bodily strength and violence of disposition a terror to the well meaning well disposed and peaceable inhabitants*". In regard to Jesse Oates, the petition went on to state "*that the said David Cogdell possessed a peculiar and rancorous hatred and without cause as your petitioners verily believe, to a certain Jesse Oates, the subject of this humble petition – that your petitioners are informed and verily believe that the said David Cogdell not only possessed positive intention but actually made public declaration of intention to put the said Jesse Oates to death when proper opportunity therefor should occur – That the said David Cogdell on the eighteenth day of September in year 1802 came to a place where the said Jesse Oates then was in perfect peace and harmony with all the world and after giving to the said Jesse the most scurous (scurrilous?) and the most unprovoked abuse, he struck him and sorry are your petitioners to be obliged to state that the temperature of mind of the said Jesse Oates prevented an appeal to the laws of his country; in the moment of immediate excitement he gave to the said Cogdell a wound of which your petitioners believe the said Cogdell afterwards died.*"[17] Despite the appeal of these men who knew both parties, the petition was rejected and Jesse Oates never returned to North Carolina. Based on this petition, it is quite possible that David Cogdell was simply a person who made it a habit of looking for trouble and found more than he bargained for.

The "written oral history" of the dispute between Jesse Oates and David Cogdell contrasts sharply with the documentary evidence and yet, like so much other oral history

---

[17] Quoted in John Martin Oates, *Roots, Seeds, and Other Things, Volume II: King-Sutton-Oates and Related Families of Duplin, Johnston, Sampson, and Wayne Counties, North Carolina* (privately printed, 1993), pp. 160-161. Like me, Oates is a descendant of both families as his Oates lineage is traceable to John Oates (brother of Jesse) and Susannah Cogdell (daughter of David Cogdell) so he has no reason for bias either.

(whether "truly oral" or "written oral") it does contain elements of truth. The petition for pardon for Jesse Oates does indicate that David Cogdell was person of "great bodily strength and violence of disposition" which fits with the oral tradition that he physically abused Jesse Oates on a regular basis. The documentation of Jethro Oates's Loyalist activities, combined with the fact that Cogdell served as a delegate to North Carolina's Constitutional Convention provide a basis for believing that the two men could have clashed over lingering Revolutionary War resentments. The author simply confused the issue over who was on which side – and given that it was the Oates family he was writing about, that is not a surprise. In the early twentieth century, very few Americans would have proudly claimed descent from Loyalists and, for that matter, they may not have known if they were. Jesse Oates himself may have concealed the truth of his father's sentiments from his children.

The facts of the situation do not reflect well on David Cogdell as an individual. Although he was clearly a supporter of the Continental cause in the American Revolution which was certainly the popular position to have taken by the early nineteenth century, contemporary documents also provide ample evidence that he was a neighborhood bully of sorts who fell victim to retribution when he harassed Jesse Oates once too often. As for Jesse's father, Jethro Oates, some descendants may take shame in his Loyalist activities in the latter stages of the War for Independence. It is hardly fair, however, to judge a man who died in 1780 when one is armed with the knowledge of how a war he did not live to see the end of actually turned out. The summer of 1780 was a low point for the Continental cause. Charleston had fallen to the British and Washington's army in the north had just suffered through the worst winter of the century. Jethro Oates and others like him had every reason to believe at that point that the British were headed toward an eventual victory. Practically, it made sense to aid the eventual winners in the hope of some compensation after the war. Whether this was Jethro Oates's motivation or if he did consistently cling to the Loyalist cause throughout the war is impossible to know. If he did, he was far from alone in that regard. If he switched sides at various points in the war, he was not alone in that either. Undoubtedly the actions he took made sense to him at the time, whatever his reasons. Some of his descendants may find the choice he made hard to understand when viewed through a lens of two centuries of subsequent history, but it is unfair to draw conclusions about him based on such standards.

Their Memories Were Imperfect, Just Like Ours

The fact that cherished family traditions may be wrong is often a bitter pill for beginning genealogists to swallow. When confronted with myth busting based on primary sources, some will have a negative reaction, believing that older family members who are no longer living are being accused of lying. That is not the case at all. How many of us accurately remember every detail of a story we were told when we were young children? Could we recite the same story, word for word, to our own children or grandchildren fifty or sixty years later? That is highly unlikely. Those of us who adopt genealogy as a serious hobby have to remember one crucial fact – the people we rely on for oral history, in most cases, did *not* make genealogy a favorite pastime. My maternal grandmother, Melba (Grogan) Williams, did have some interest in it and the stories she told me of her own parents when I was a child helped spark my own interest. She never, however, looked up anything in a county courthouse or made a trip to the State Archives. My paternal grandmother, Jessie (Bagley) Hite, still remembered some of the names she had compiled for her childhood school project, but she had no real interest in learning more and seemed puzzled at my enthusiasm. She was, however, taken aback when I informed her that her Bush ancestors had been English rather than Dutch. My maternal grandmother was no longer lucid by the time I learned that her Carter ancestors were not from the same family as Robert E. Lee's mother – but I am quite certain that if she had been, she would not have been pleased to hear it. My mother probably would have discouraged me from telling her.

They Didn't Ask for Documentation

Perhaps Elizabeth Warren summed it up as well as anyone in a campaign ad she produced in response to questions about her alleged Native American heritage. She said "As a kid, I never asked my mom for documentation when she talked about our Native American heritage. What kid would?" Warren is absolutely right about that in most cases. To take it a step further, what adult would ask for documentation of such a tradition? The answer to that is simple – an adult who adopts genealogy as a major pastime would ask such a question. Other adults would not, not even serious scholars, unless they happened to have a significant interest in genealogy. Warren, a law professor at Harvard University, is certainly an accomplished scholar in her own field, but she probably never undertook a serious study of her own genealogy – like most Americans, she accepted what she was told by her parents. Gerald Posner, also a serious scholar, also never turned to primary sources for the genealogy of James Earl Ray, the subject of one of his books. He was apparently unaware of the types of public records that are available even on the poorest of families and therefore took the word of Ray's father that the family descended from Ned Ray who was hanged in modern-day Montana in 1864. Thomas Flynn, the editor of *Free Inquiry* and another accomplished scholar, took it for granted that the 1926 genealogy of the Ingersoll family in New England was correct in citing two unrelated Ingersoll immigrants as brothers. As with Warren and Posner, genealogy is probably not an area of expertise for him and he would not be likely to know what types of primary sources to check to confirm or refute established traditions in genealogy.

For most of us, the people who were our sources of oral history were not scholars the caliber of Elizabeth Warren, Gerald Posner, and Thomas Flynn. But like these three, they did not research primary sources before passing on the oral traditions we heard from them. They probably lacked the time, the means, the interest, or all three. We all have to remember that when we learn that things they told us are not perfectly accurate, we should not assume they deliberately lied to us – or that their parents or grandparents deliberately lied to them. Deliberate falsification cannot always be entirely ruled out in certain cases, such as a denial of German heritage by a veteran of either World War or a substitution of a Native American ancestor for an African one by a white Southerner. In most cases, though, inaccurate information is a result of a less-than-perfect memory of stories heard many years before. The more generations a tradition has passed through before it reaches the ears of a serious genealogist (or is committed to paper as "written oral history"), the more likely it is that it includes some distortions.

What Might I Have Missed?

I sometimes shudder to think of all the inaccuracies I might still believe if I had accepted all of the oral traditions I heard without question. I might still be searching for my Hite ancestors among 19th century Dutch immigrants or attempting to connect them to 17th century New Netherland. I might still be searching for a Dutchman named Van den Bosch or a German named Busch who fathered a son named Joshua in Pennsylvania in the 1790s. I might have recorded that my great-great-grandmother, Catherine Ann (Thrawls) Hite was the daughter of a German immigrant named John Thrawls and an unidentified Native American woman he married soon after his arrival in this country. I might have latched onto James Stuart, supposedly born about 1851 in Wythe County, Virginia as the father of my great-grandmother, Mary Ella (Stewart) Grogan (said to have been a native of Wythe County but actually born in Stokes County, North Carolina). I might still believe that my Carter ancestors were from the same family as Robert E. Lee. But what makes me shudder even more is to think of all of the things I might never have known if I had taken oral history for granted. I might never have located my Hite (Heidt/Heyd) family's village of origin in Germany, much less visited it and met some distant cousins there. I might not have located my English Bush ancestors in Enfield, Connecticut and all of the other ancestral families associated with that line that came to that town from northeastern Massachusetts in the early 1680s. I might not have located Mary (Hiestand) Huff, a married woman who somehow defied conventions in 1830 by taking a land patent in her own right in Harrison County, Ohio. I might have clung to the belief that one of my King ancestors was a sibling of William Rufus King and thus never known of my connections to the quarrelsome David Cogdell , the Loyalist Jethro Oates, or the Revolutionary War soldier Willis Wiggins.

In September of 2012, I visited the Oblong Meeting House in Pawling, New York – about a three hour trip from my home in Providence. This structure, a Quaker meeting house, was built in 1764, though the meeting in that area dated back at least a generation before that time. I had only recently learned that the building still existed though I had long known that one set of my 4th great-grandparents, James and Hannah (Hoag) Sherman, both born in the early 1770s, had grown up attending that meeting. They had left Pawling shortly after their marriage and moved to Queensbury, New York, where their daughter Matilda was born in 1798. Matilda was the source of one of those "awful names" that my great-grandmother, Matilda Lovisa (Bush) Bagley had been "stuck with" according to her daughter (my grandmother). Matilda Sherman married Moses Hambleton in 1816 in Ellery, New York (where her parents had moved a few years earlier) and their daughter Mary Hambleton, born in 1823, was the mother of Matilda Lovisa Bush.

While visiting the Oblong Meeting House and the local library, I learned that the meeting had, in 1767, raised the question of whether it was "consistent with the Christian spirit to hold a person in slavery at all." Nine years later, the meeting reached the conclusion that it would no longer accept financial contributions nor receive services from any Friends (Quakers) holding slaves. Some literature on the Oblong Meeting House claims that it was the first religious body in the American colonies to take that step. All four of Matilda Sherman's grandparents were members of that meeting when the discussion began – Joshua and Mary (Soule) Sherman on her father's side and David and Martha (Haviland) Hoag on her mother's side. Some of her great-grandparents were also living at the time and undoubtedly participated in the discussion – George Soule, David Hoag, Sr., and Isaac and Elizabeth (Bates) Haviland. Seeing the meeting house where my ancestors participated in such a significant discussion (whether or not the claim of being the "first" is actually true) was one of the highlights of my many adventures in genealogy-related travels.

Through some of these Quakers associated with the Oblong Meeting, I am a descendant of several supporters of Anne Hutchinson, who was expelled from the Massachusetts Bay colony after the Antinomian Controversy of the mid-1630s – Philip and Sarah (Odding) Sherman, John and Mary Coggeshall, and Nicholas Easton – all of whom were forced out of Massachusetts Bay along with Hutchinson and relocated to Aquidneck Island, now part of the state of Rhode Island. Easton and the Shermans later converted to Quakerism and Easton served as Governor of the colony from 1673 until his death two years later. It is also through this lineage that I am a descendant of the Mayflower passenger George Soule (great-grandfather of the aforementioned George Soule). These are all people I never would have identified as ancestors had I accepted my initial instinct that James Hamilton of Venango County, Pennsylvania was my ancestor. The ancestors of Matilda's husband Moses Hambleton (who *replaced* James Hamilton, so to speak, as Mary Hambleton's actual father) are no less interesting. He was a descendant of no fewer than three Quaker couples, perhaps more, who arrived in Pennsylvania from England in 1682, the very first year of Quaker settlement of the new colony – Nicholas and Jane (Turner) Waln, James and Jane (Gurden) Paxson, and George and Eleanor Pownall. Moses's ancestors also include some Germans – the Küster family who were among the very first Germans to arrive in Pennsylvania. These are more ancestors I could have missed out on identifying had I ignored my grandmother and accepted James Hamilton of Venango County, Pennsylvania as a great-great-great-grandfather.

Jessie (Bagley) Hite could not have cared less about any of the ancestors I located. If anything, she may have been dismayed to learn of the Mayflower connection. She occasionally spoke of a man she worked with prior to her marriage whose surname was Alden. I can still hear the disgust in her voice "ninth-generation direct descendant of John Alden and Priscilla Mullins and he didn't let you forget it either!" She had a definite distaste for hereditary organizations such as the Society of Mayflower Descendants and the Daughters of the American Revolution. My maternal grandmother, Melba (Grogan) Williams, was more interested in family history, though she never did any primary source research to my knowledge. I am quite certain she would have been disturbed by my discoveries that some of the traditions she grew up hearing were inaccurate – such as the alleged link to the mother of Robert E. Lee. I am also certain she would have been shocked at the documentation of the voluntary surrender of her grandfather, Charles Grogan, to Union forces at Spotsylvania. I would like to believe that some of the other discoveries I have made about her ancestors – people like Edward and Unity Harris (even though Unity was certainly *not* a Native American), the Revolutionary War soldier George Martin and his wife Mary (Bailey) Martin and some others that have not been mentioned in this work – would make up for that. None of those people were as prominent as the Carter relatives of Robert E. Lee but they were, in my opinion, no less interesting.

CPSIA information can be obtained at www.ICGtesting.com
Printed in the USA
BVOW04s0354050514

352491BV00012B/211/P